LEADER'S GUIDE
FOR CY AND CY NANO

CY Leader's Guide (2nd Edition)
Copyright © 2010 Christianity Explored

www.christianityexplored.org

Published by
The Good Book Company Ltd
Elm House, 37 Elm Road, New Malden, Surrey KT3 3HB, UK
Tel: 0845-225-0880; International: +44 (0) 208 942 0880
Email: admin@thegoodbook.co.uk

Websites:
UK: www.thegoodbook.co.uk
N America: www.thegoodbook.com
Australia: www.thegoodbook.com.au
New Zealand: www.thegoodbook.co.nz

CHRISTIANITY
E✝PLORED

ISBN: 9781907377136

Design by Steve Devane and André Parker

Printed in the UK

Welcome TO CY

Welcome to *CY*, the youth edition of *Christianity Explored*.

This seven-week course is designed to present young people with the good news about Jesus. With a creative mixture of Bible studies, talks, DVDs, activities and group discussions, CY takes your youth group on a journey through Mark's Gospel. They'll discover the identity, mission and call of Jesus on their lives – who Jesus is, what he came to do, and how he calls us to respond.

This course, now in its second edition, has benefitted enormously from the experience of the many youth leaders in churches worldwide that have led thousands of young people through the material, and brought them face to face with the gospel of Jesus Christ.

Today, as always, young people of all ages need to hear the message of forgiveness, hope, meaning and purpose that will bring a shape to their lives, and a new relationship with God that will last for eternity.

What makes this course – and the Christian gospel – distinctive is its insistence on God's remarkable grace: the clear teaching that although we human beings have rebelled against God, we are deeply loved by him. Loved with an outrageous, costly and incomprehensible love that was poured out for us on a little hill just outside Jerusalem.

It may be no easier for leaders to explain Jesus' teaching on sin, judgment, wrath and hell than it is for the young people to hear it. But, if we are prepared to trust in the Holy Spirit's power to open blind eyes, these uncomfortable truths pave the way for a faithful, fruitful life driven by God's grace.

This Leader's Guide is divided into four sections: the first will introduce you to how the course works and train you to run it; the second will be your guide session by session as you run the CY Nano course for 11-14s; the third will guide you in running CY for 15+ and young adults; and the fourth section contains session outlines and programme suggestions for the *Inside Track* weekend/day away.

If you are running a CY course of any kind, please log onto **www.christianityexplored.org** and register it, so that others may pray for you, or even send other people along.

Contents

SECTION 3: STUDY GUIDE FOR CY (15+)

SECTION 4: *INSIDE TRACK* WEEKEND/DAY AWAY

APPENDICES: *ANSWERING DIFFICULT QUESTIONS*

How to run
the course

Getting started

Telling young people about Jesus Christ is a stunning privilege and a huge responsibility. It's a stunning privilege because Almighty God is pleased to call us his "fellow workers" (1 Corinthians 3:9) as he seeks and saves the lost. And it's a huge responsibility because it can be tempting to present a watered-down gospel that has no power to save and is "no gospel at all" (Galatians 1:7). Our evangelism, especially with impressionable young people, must always be careful, prayerful and faithful.

CY has been developed to let the gospel tell the gospel: it takes you, and those in your care, on a seven-session journey through Mark's Gospel to discover who Jesus is, why he came and what it means to follow him.

To help your journey run smoothly, you will need to consider the following before the course begins.

WHO WILL COME?

For many churches with an existing work among teenagers and young adults, the first place to start is the groups that you have running week by week. Running CY or CY Nano need not be billed as a specifically evangelistic course – it may be billed as a "refresher course" on the basics of the Christian message, or simply as a series that goes through Mark's Gospel. So even for those who have some kind of Christian commitment, there will be plenty of spiritual "meat" in the course, as they study the Bible together and think about the message of Christianity.

And there is great value in running this course "internally" to begin with.

- **Teaching:** The gospel is not only how you come to faith in Christ, it is also the means by which you grow in your understanding of God, and your love for him. CY *teaches* the gospel over seven sessions in a way which will be fresh and accessible to your group, and build their understanding and faith.

- **Inreach:** Any group will have members or fringe members who are not yet Christians. CY is an evangelistic tool to explain the gospel of Christ to them.

- **Training:** If you hope at some stage to use CY as a specific outreach tool, then running it first with your professing Christians will train them and your other leaders in how it works, and inspire them to invite others the next time it is run.

Obviously, we would hope that CY goes on to be used more formally as an outreach programme, where group members are specifically invited to join in order to discover more about what it means to be a Christian today. These kinds of groups will vary enormously, depending on the age group CY is used with, and the context in which it happens. So, for example, you may be running it in a home, or on school or college premises in a lunchtime, or on church premises on a weekend, or at another "neutral" venue.

We have written the course material to include ideas for a variety of settings and groups, but you must adapt the material to suit your particular group and circumstances.

WHERE SHOULD YOU MEET?

Find somewhere where your group will be happy to invite their friends. You may like to experiment with some different locations other than church premises. Avoid using a classroom or somewhere that looks like one so that people don't feel they are back in school. The aim is to create a relational environment where people can listen to the Bible teaching while they enjoy the warmth of Christian fellowship so that they feel sufficiently relaxed to ask their questions and express their doubts and feelings.

The physical environment where you run CY can have a big impact on people's willingness to get involved in activities and discussion, so be creative in the way you decorate and set up the room. It's important to choose a place where you are unlikely to be interrupted and where you will be able to meet every week at the same time.

HOW OFTEN SHOULD YOU MEET?

As this is a seven-session course, once a week for seven weeks is the ideal. Because each week builds on the one before, try not to interrupt the regular schedule of the meetings.

There's also a weekend or day away that we suggest takes place between Weeks 6 and 7, called *Inside Track*. The material relating to this is in section 4 at the back of this handbook. The idea of this weekend/day away material is to give group members an insight into what it means to live as a Christian – and therefore what would be involved if they decided to follow Christ themselves.

WHY SEVEN WEEKS?

In some youth evangelism there has been too much emphasis on a prepackaged gospel presentation which aims to "get people to pray the prayer", often with little opportunity for serious consideration of what is involved in following Jesus. This approach to evangelism can be valid when you are dealing with people who already have the building blocks for understanding the gospel in place – knowing the facts about Jesus' life, death and resurrection, understanding the Christian view of God, etc. But increasingly, young people either have no understanding of these things, or else have knowledge that is patchy or confused. That is why this course seeks to put in place the building blocks of understanding the gospel slowly, over several weeks, with plenty of room for discussion and reflection.

As Christians, our aim should be to work for "fruit that will last" (John 15:16), not a superficial religious experience that is quickly forgotten when life gets tough. With that in mind, CY clearly sets out the implications of becoming a Christian, so that young people can adequately "count the cost" before making a commitment.

WHAT'S INVOLVED IN EACH SESSION?

The structure we suggest is the same for each session:

1. Group activity;

2. EXPLORE (Bible study);

3. Talk or DVD;

4. TALKBACK (group discussion).

When this is packaged up with some time for food or just general hanging around time, it gives rise to a two-hour programme as below. Alternatively, a stripped down version can be done in an hour. Below are some suggested timings in minutes for each component:

Full programme		Shorter programme	
Food	30	Introduction	5
Group activity	25	Group activity	10
Explore	20	Explore	10
Talk/DVD	15-20	Talk/DVD	15
Talkback	25	Talkback	20
TOTAL	**120**	**TOTAL**	**60**

You should be able to complete the full programme for a session in less than 2 hours. This can be shortened if necessary by limiting the time taken for food, activities or discussion. It is important to watch the time used for each of these components. Over-running can cause frustration and boredom – and may make it difficult for you to communicate the gospel effectively. CY has been extensively piloted with groups all over the world and the current course is the result of detailed feedback. We would urge you, when you first run the course, to try and use it as written – you may be surprised by how well your group handles the activities and questions!

FOOD
The main reason that food is suggested as part of the programme is not as a device to get young people to come (although in our experience, teenagers and students will go anywhere for a free feed!). Rather, it is because as you sit or stand around eating, you and your fellow leaders have the opportunity to interact with the young people – to discover what they are like, what interests them, what struggles and difficulties they face.

Time is precious, so if you can, recruit outside help with the food so that you are free to spend time with the group members. Resist the temptation to make the food over-elaborate. Keep it simple to eat and clear away. (Although it's always good to make an effort, there is a danger that food can end up squeezing out time for exploring the gospel.)

GROUP ACTIVITY
This is a short, fun game, intended to introduce the theme of the session, and build relationships between people. Each time you meet you will need to make sure you have all the equipment needed to run the activity, and have thought through how it will work for your particular group, in the place you are running CY.

EXPLORE

This is a Bible study from Mark's Gospel, giving the group a chance to explore Jesus' life and teaching.

The skill of your fellow leaders is crucial during EXPLORE – an excellent reason for you to schedule some training time with them. You will find extensive notes on training later on in this section.

TALK OR DVD

At this point you, as the course leader, will deliver a short talk based on a passage from the Gospel of Mark. Alternatively, you can use the *Soul* DVD instead of doing a "live" talk for the seven main CY sessions. There is no DVD material for the *Inside Track* material, so you will have to do live talks for them.

If you are using the *Soul* DVD, make sure that your leaders have watched the episode beforehand so that there will be no surprises with the content. Because the DVDs feature on-screen Bible text, it is inadvisable to use them with large groups unless you have access to a projection screen and projector.

TALKBACK

This is a chance to discuss the themes of the talk, and bring out the implications. TALKBACK questions are particularly designed to draw out what your group members actually believe.

HOW WILL YOU INVITE PEOPLE?

If you are running CY as an outreach series, then you will need to encourage your group to invite their friends. You might want to do a study with them on the importance of evangelism before you start running CY – although the best way to motivate your regulars to bring others on the course is for them to experience it themselves first. "Friends bringing friends" is the main reason people come to the course.

If you are running CY as part of a church youth group, you should advertise the course in your church bulletin, during the Sunday services, and at your regular youth group meetings.

Any publicity material you produce about the course needs to reassure people that no one will be expected to pray, sing or do anything that makes them feel uncomfortable or embarrassed. It is also important to be honest about exactly what will happen, so that people don't feel duped into coming.

It is our hope that the course would not be a "one-time" event, but rather become a regular feature of your calendar. And once your youth group have experienced CY, you'll find that they'll be eager to invite their friends to future courses.

WHO WILL LEAD?

We recommend that one leader is made responsible for delivering all the talks, or introducing the DVDs, and running the whole session. If the group is small, the same leader will lead the group through EXPLORE and TALKBACK.

If you have a large group, you will need to split participants into smaller discussion groups and find additional leaders to lead EXPLORE and TALKBACK with each group. Participants should stay with the same leader(s) every week. We recommend a maximum of 8 young people per group, with at least two leaders per group.

All leaders should be Christians who are able to teach, encourage discussion and care for participants. They should be able to teach the Bible faithfully and clearly – and be able to deal with difficult questions on Mark's Gospel (see page 197).

Participants may have questions that are not explicitly dealt with in the material, so leaders should have enough general biblical knowledge to help participants with these questions. (For help on answering difficult questions, see the section at the back of this manual and visit www.christianityexplored.org/reading)

Leaders should also be able to handle pastoral situations with care and sensitivity. In a mixed group, it is vital to have both male and female leaders present, in order to deal with pastoral situations appropriately. It can be very effective to ask Christian young people to help lead the course. The most important qualities of a leader are not age, but maturity in their understanding and gifting.

Asking a suitable young person to lead may encourage greater discussion and debate. If you do take this route, having an older Christian present in the group (but not leading the discussion) will be helpful in dealing with difficult situations or hard questions. It's also a good idea to choose a young leader who has already been through CY as a participant.

WHAT WILL YOU NEED TO RUN CY?

Everyone on the course – leaders and participants – will need to be given a Bible, or the Gospel of Mark. For the sake of clarity, it is important that everyone uses the same version. The version used throughout the course material is the New International Version (NIV). If you choose to use another version, please check carefully that the wording of the questions makes sense against the Bible version you are using.

An NIV Gospel of Mark themed for the *Soul* DVD is available to buy. Participants will only need Mark during the main seven sessions, but will need full Bibles for the *Inside Track* studies during the weekend/day away.

Each participant should be given a copy of the *CY* or *CY Nano Handbook,* which contains the EXPLORE studies, space to write their answers, talk summaries (Downloads) and room to make notes. We recommend that, for a younger group, these are kept by the leaders and handed out each week. (When you collect them after TALKBACK, you will need to promise that their Handbooks are private and that the leaders won't be reading them! Explain that you're holding on to them so that they won't be forgotten next week.)

HOW SHOULD YOU PRAY FOR CY?

Nothing happens unless God is at work, so make sure that you give plenty of time to prayer. Try to recruit prayer partners among your Christian friends, or from your church congregation, who will commit themselves to praying before (and during) the course.

- **Pray for the preparation of the talks** – that they would be faithful to God's word, passionate, challenging and clear.

- **Pray for the leaders** – that they would be well prepared and that they would "watch their life and doctrine closely" (1 Timothy 4:16).

- **Pray for the young people themselves** – that many would attend; that by his Spirit, God would open their eyes to see who Jesus is, and by his Spirit give them the desire to turn and follow him.

explore

4

CY Jesus died

Imagine you know how and when you will die. How would it make you feel? What would it make you do?

READ MARK 8:27–33

What does Peter realize in verse 29?

Why would Jesus' words in verse 31 surprise Peter?

Why does Jesus confront Peter in verse 33?

When Jesus died on the cross, was it unexpected? (Look at Mark 9:31 and Mark 10:33–34 for clues.)

17

Please let us know when and where your course is running! The CY Team would love to pray for you. Email cy@christianityexplored.org or register your course at **www.christianityexplored.org**

Why tell young people the gospel?

Why would anyone want to run a course on Mark's Gospel with a group of young people?

We all know that youth work is hard. There are heartaches, disappointments and difficulties. Surely it would be better to provide games and entertainment for young people and then try to reach them when they are older? But by that time, of course, if entertainment is all we've offered them, they will have long since found better entertainment elsewhere. It is, after all, something the world specializes in!

But as Christians, we can offer our young people something much more profound and compelling than entertainment, something that the world cannot compete with. We can share with them the gospel of God.

And when the gospel is presented in all its fullness, young lives can be changed by God radically and miraculously – forever. Although reaching young people with the gospel of Jesus Christ and training them to be committed disciples can be hard, it is also an extraordinarily joyful task – it is something worth spending your life on.

1. GOD DESIRES THAT YOUNG PEOPLE SHOULD KNOW HIM

The writer of Ecclesiastes considers what life is like when every possible pleasure is indulged – but God is excluded. He reaches a simple conclusion:

> *"Remember your Creator in the days of your youth."*
> Ecclesiastes 12:1

We should be mindful of our Creator when we are young. Sometimes we view the teenage years of young people as a phase that must be passed through before we can focus on winning them to Christ. Provided they get through those difficult years without getting into too many unhelpful things, and keep coming to church once in a while, we are content. But God wants young people to know him and be in a living relationship with him.

2. THE TIME TO KNOW GOD IS WHEN WE ARE YOUNG

The writer of Ecclesiastes reflects that it is better to know God *"before the days of trouble come and the years approach when you will say, 'I find no pleasure in them'"* (12:1).

Why is that so? Because knowing God from our youth gives us reason and purpose for the rest of our lives. We live the life we were intended to live. Equally, God does not want us to waste the years he has given us. He wants us to use them for him, taking "pleasure in them" by serving him.

Great leaders are often formed when they are young. King David knew and served God from a young age; Daniel followed God from youth and Timothy was reminded by Paul that he had been taught about God from his youth.

When God saves a young person, he uses their youth to form them, to mould their character and attitudes, to shape a person who will follow Jesus for the rest of their lives – and influence others to do the same.

Think of what a difference a young person could make living fully for Jesus Christ: their witness at school; all the friends they can reach; the salt and light that they can be in a lost world. The young people of today are the serving, growing Christians of tomorrow and even the leaders of the future.

If we invest our lives and energies in young people, we are investing in those who have the potential to love and glorify God for decades to come.

3. IF WE WAIT IT COULD BE TOO LATE
At the end of chapter 12, the writer of Ecclesiastes urges us to remember our Creator *"before the silver cord is severed, or the golden bowl is broken"* (v 6) and *"the dust returns to the ground it came from, and the spirit returns to God who gave it"* (v 7).

These are pictures of death. But it is not only the old who die; sometimes the young die too. And ultimately, everyone – whether young or old – will face death and the judgment of God.

So we must share the gospel with young people before it is too late.

4. IT IS A TIME OF GREAT GOSPEL OPPORTUNITY
Statistics (mainly from the USA) tell us that as many as 85% of all Christians say they made a commitment to Christ between the ages of 4 and 14. A further 10% would say they started their Christian lives between the ages of 15 and 30. This means that the effectiveness of evangelism is greater with young people and students than at any other time in their lives. Some missional thinkers refer to this as the "4-14 window".

This means that, as youth leaders, you are in the forefront of the most effective evangelistic opportunity you will have. Make good use of it!

5. IT IS THE COMMAND OF THE LORD JESUS
Jesus commanded his followers to go into the world and make disciples of all nations (Matthew 28:19-20). That task includes young people. Notice that our aim is not just to preach the gospel and move on. It is to *make disciples,* in just the same way that Jesus made disciples. He spent time with them, taught them, discussed questions with them and encouraged them in the first stirrings of their faith in him. The pattern we are to follow in making disciples is the same.

God's role in evangelism – and ours

We need to distinguish between God's role in evangelism and our role. It's going to be incredibly frustrating if we try to perform God's role – because only the Creator of the universe is able to do that. Look at 2 Corinthians 4:1–6.

> "Therefore, since through God's mercy we have this ministry, we do not lose heart. Rather, we have renounced secret and shameful ways; we do not use deception, nor do we distort the word of God. On the contrary, by setting forth the truth plainly we commend ourselves to every man's conscience in the sight of God. And even if our gospel is veiled, it is veiled to those who are perishing. The god of this age has blinded the minds of unbelievers, so that they cannot see the light of the gospel of the glory of Christ, who is the image of God. For we do not preach ourselves, but Jesus Christ as Lord, and ourselves as your servants for Jesus' sake. For God, who said, 'Let light shine out of darkness,' made his light shine in our hearts to give us the light of the knowledge of the glory of God in the face of Christ."

GOD'S ROLE IN EVANGELISM

What is God's role in evangelism? God makes "his light shine in our hearts to give us the light of the knowledge of the glory of God in the face of Christ".

In other words, God enables us to recognize that Jesus is God. God makes it possible – by his Holy Spirit – for a person to see who Jesus is.

The beginning of 2 Corinthians 4:6 reminds us that God said, "Let light shine out of darkness." That is a reference to the miracle of creation in Genesis 1:3. This same God, who brought light into the world at creation, now shines light into the hearts of human beings, enabling them to see that Jesus is God. In other words, for people to recognize that Jesus is God, God must perform a miracle.

People do not become Christians just because we share the gospel with them. God must shine his light in people's hearts so that they recognize and respond to the truth of the gospel.

And we know from verse 4 that people can't see the truth of the gospel because "the god of this age has blinded the minds of unbelievers".

Here, Paul reminds us that we are in the middle of a supernatural battlefield. The reason so many reject the gospel is that the devil is at work, preventing people from recognizing who Jesus is.

The devil blinds people by making them chase after the things of this world, which are passing away and which cannot save them. Their concerns are confined to the here and now: their popularity, their family, their relationships, their material possessions. They are blind to anything beyond that.

As a result, they can only see Jesus in the here and now, perhaps as a great moral teacher; his eternal significance is completely obscured. And, according to verse 4, Satan is determined to prevent people from seeing "the light of the gospel of the glory of Christ, who is the image of God". Satan does not want people to recognize who Jesus is.

OUR ROLE IN EVANGELISM

What then is our role in evangelism? *"We ... preach ... Jesus Christ as Lord"*.

The word "preach" can evoke negative images, but it derives from a word simply meaning "herald", someone who relates important announcements from the king to his kingdom. Our role is to tell people the gospel and leave the Spirit of God to convict them of its truth.

These verses also reveal the attitude we should adopt as we preach. We are to be like "servants for Jesus' sake". The word translated "servants" literally means "slaves" in Greek. Paul was determined to present Christ to others without any hint of self-promotion.

We must remember that the only difference between ourselves and an unbeliever is that God, in his mercy, has opened our blind eyes and illuminated our hearts by his Holy Spirit. We should be forever grateful, and so seek to promote Christ, not ourselves.

We must keep preaching Christ as Lord and, remembering that only a miracle from God can open blind eyes, we must keep praying that God will shine his light in the hearts of unbelievers.

2 Corinthians 4:1–6 also helps us to carry out our role in the right way: *"we do not use deception, nor do we distort the word of God... by setting forth the truth plainly we commend ourselves to every man's conscience in the sight of God ... For we do not preach ourselves, but Jesus Christ as Lord."*

When we tell people about Christ, we should demonstrate the following qualities:

- ❯ **Integrity** – *"we do not use deception"*. We are straight with people; we are genuine and sincere, and we never use any kind of emotional manipulation.

- ❯ **Fidelity** – we do not *"distort the word of God"*. We have to tell people the tough bits. If – for example – we don't tell our young people about sin, about hell, and about the necessity of repentance, then we are distorting God's word. Preaching these hard truths means trusting in the work of the Holy Spirit to draw people to Christ, however "difficult" the message.

- ❯ **Humility** – *"we do not preach ourselves, but Jesus Christ as Lord"*. We must draw people to Jesus, not to ourselves. We must always remember that young people are easily impressionable, and that we want them to make a decision to follow Christ because they are convinced by the truth, and are being led by the Holy Spirit, rather than being manipulated by their admiration of the youth leader.

As we use CY to preach the gospel, we must remember that it is up to God whether somebody becomes a Christian or not. Only he can open blind eyes, so we must trust him for the results. God will do his part, and we must do ours.

How the course works

During this seven-session course, as Mark's Gospel is read and taught, you will be helping young people to explore three questions that cut right to the heart of Christianity:

- Who was Jesus?

- Why did Jesus come?

- What does Jesus demand of those who want to follow him?

In other words, the course is all about:

- Jesus' identity

- Jesus' mission

- Jesus' call.

The first six sessions focus on Jesus' identity and mission. In particular, your group will explore the problem of sin and the wonder of forgiveness. There is then the *Inside Track* weekend or day away, when participants are given a deeper insight into what it means to be a follower of Christ – and are assured that God will graciously provide his Holy Spirit, the church family, the Bible and prayer to uphold them.

The objective in the final week is to emphasize Christ's call in Mark 8:34: "If anyone would come after me, he must deny himself and take up his cross and follow me".

The CY programme is built on the conviction that the gospel must be taught slowly and carefully, and that we allow the Gospel (of Mark) to tell the gospel of Jesus Christ. The content of the gospel message is important to get right. Many evangelistic programmes respond to the changing interests and felt needs of the hearers, and tragically end up with something that is appealing, but has no power to save. CY is unafraid to put centre stage many issues and doctrines that have been watered down in some gospel presentations: the identity of Jesus Christ as the Son of God; the problem of sin and our need for forgiveness; the reality of the coming judgment; and the substitutionary death of Jesus Christ on the cross. The table on the next page gives an overview of the course content.

Effective evangelism usually happens within the context of the gospel message being delivered by people who model its meaning effectively. Paul talks about how our character and works can "make the teaching about God our Saviour attractive" (Titus 2:10). It is important to get the content of the gospel right. It is equally important that those who lead on CY are people who have been themselves transformed by the love of Christ.

	Explore	CY Nano Talk	CY/Soul DVD	Talkback
Week 1	Mark 1:1	CY it's worth exploring	Christianity is Christ	Discuss talk
Week 2	Mark 2:1-12	CY Jesus matters	Identity	Discuss talk
Week 3	Mark 12:28-31	CY Jesus came	Mission	Discuss talk
Week 4	Mark 8:27-33	CY Jesus died	Cross	Discuss talk
Week 5	Mark 15:42 – 16:8	CY Jesus lives	Resurrection	Discuss talk
Week 6	Mark 10:17-22	CY God accepts us	Grace	Discuss talk
Inside Track		CY you need the Holy Spirit CY the church is your family CY it's good to talk		Discuss talk
Week 7	Mark 1:14-15	CY we should believe	Call	Discuss talk

THE MARK CHALLENGE

At the back of the CY and CY Nano Handbooks is a page called "The Mark Challenge". It's basically a reading plan which will take someone through the whole of the Gospel of Mark in three weeks. As well as looking in detail at smaller sections of Mark in the CY sessions, you may want to encourage your group to pick up *The Mark Challenge* to read right the way through the Gospel during the time they are doing CY. It may therefore be appropriate to include some time during each session to ask people to feed back questions, thoughts or comments on what they have been reading in Mark throughout the week. But be careful that this does not turn into "Bible-study overkill".

Throughout the course, as you communicate the gospel to your young people, here are some things to keep in mind.

GET TO KNOW THEM

Young people place enormous emphasis on relationships, so get to know them as well as you can. This doesn't mean that youth work involves "becoming like" young people, but it does mean that youth work is about taking time to get to know them as people.

GET ALONGSIDE THEM

One way to develop a relationship with a young person is to get alongside them through what they enjoy doing outside school. Whether it be sports or computer games, look to get into the world of a young person. Find out what makes them tick and, if it is wholesome, get to know them through it.

DON'T BE AFRAID TO HAVE FUN WITH THEM

Show them that you are a real person and are able to relax with them.

TAKE AN INTEREST

Many parents think that teenagers are a nuisance and most adults steer clear of young people, but if you show that you care about them and are interested in them as individuals, that will go a long way towards getting the gospel across.

It is worth mentioning that although it appears natural, talking about their school day is probably not the favourite subject of a young person and so may be worth avoiding!

AS FAR AS POSSIBLE, TREAT THEM AS ADULTS

During the course, your young people will be asked to discuss serious subjects with maturity, so, as far as you are able, treat them as adults.

However, discipline problems can emerge when working with young people. If you do face a difficult individual or situation, try the following:

- ❯ Be clear about what is acceptable and unacceptable in that situation. Young people appreciate clarity. (It is probably not a good idea to set out general "ground-rules" at the start of the course, as they may feel as if they are back at school.)

- ❯ Take them to one side and don't confront them in front of their friends. Describe what they are doing and why it is a problem.

- ❯ Don't be afraid to deal with a problem if someone or something becomes a constant distraction. Few people enjoy confrontation, but if someone is disrupting a discussion, you need to remember that they are jeopardizing a gospel opportunity.

ABOVE ALL, TREAT THEM WITH CARE

You need to be aware that your friendliness is open to misinterpretation by young people and their parents. Make sure that there is not *even a hint … of any kind of impurity* (Ephesians 5:3) in anything you do or say. It is unwise to speak alone with a young person out of view of other people, even if you are praying with them.

In addition, there will also be health and safety and child protection laws that you'll need to be familiar with. Make sure you know what these are and stick to them.

Before the course

A well-prepared CY leader will be dedicated in two particular areas: they'll be dedicated to the Bible and dedicated to prayer.

DEDICATED TO THE BIBLE

The Bible is God's word. Whenever we open the Bible, God addresses us. In Hebrews 4:12 we read: *"For the word of God is living and active. Sharper than any double-edged sword, it penetrates even to dividing soul and spirit, joints and marrow; it judges the thoughts and attitudes of the heart."* Nothing else can do this.

Because we're convinced of the power of God's word, our focus should always be on opening the Bible with young people.

DEDICATED TO PRAYER

Paul encourages the Christians at Colosse to devote themselves to prayer – in particular to pray for him in his evangelism. In Colossians 4:2-3 he says, *"Devote yourselves to prayer, being watchful and thankful. And pray for us, too, that God may open a door for our message."* Before, during and after the course, we must pray.

Mobilize others to pray too. Evangelism is a spiritual battle, so ask other Christians to pray for you and for your group. Report back to them regularly so that they can pray for specific needs and be encouraged by answered prayer.

With those two points in mind, there are a number of things you should do before the course starts.

GET TO KNOW MARK'S GOSPEL, THE HANDBOOK AND THE DVD

Read Mark at least three times and familiarize yourself with the Handbook that your group will be using, and the guidance on the answers to questions in the relevant section of this book. You will feel much more confident to lead participants once you've prepared yourself for the Bible studies and discussions that make up the course.

As your group members read through Mark, you will need to be prepared to answer any questions they come up with that arise from the Bible text. There is a section on page 197 that will help you with this. You will need to study and absorb this.

If you are using them, watch each episode of the *Soul* DVD through several times. This will help you to become more familiar with the material, and also enable you to refer back to it during discussion. *"Do you remember what was said in the DVD...?"*

GET TO KNOW YOUR FELLOW LEADERS

It is important that people not only hear the gospel explained clearly, but also see it modelled in the life of believers. You will be praying together, studying together, and teaching young people together, so it's important to get to know each other and pray for each other before you begin. Your unity and love for one another will speak volumes about the truth of the gospel message.

PREPARE YOUR TESTIMONY

"Always be prepared to give an answer to everyone who asks you to give the reason for the hope that you have. But do this with gentleness and respect" (1 Peter 3:15).

A testimony is an account of God's work in your life. Everybody who has been born again and who is becoming like Christ has a unique, interesting and powerful testimony, regardless of whether or not it appears spectacular. At some point during the course, you may feel it appropriate to share your testimony with the group. Often someone will ask you directly how you became a Christian and you will want to have an answer ready. There are specific opportunities for sharing your experience of what it is like to be a Christian built into the *Inside Track* material, but you should be ready to give an answer about the hope you have in you at any time.

> **Focus it:** Keep pointing to Christ, not yourself.

> **Structure it:** It may help to plan your testimony under these headings:

>> *My background (something about your family and how that shaped you);*

>> *How I used to think (don't dwell so much on the sinful things you used to do, but rather on what you believed about God, the world, and yourself);*

>> *How I heard the gospel and my reaction to it;*

>> *How God changed me (how you responded to Jesus' call).*

> **Personalize it:** Include one or two personal anecdotes to bring it to life. Keep it honest and interesting.

> **Time it**: Keep it short – if it's over 3 minutes, it's probably too long!

PREPARE FOR DIFFICULT QUESTIONS

The course starts by asking the group members to answer this question: *"If you could ask God one question … what would it be?"* This will throw up a huge number of questions that will need careful handling. The appendices, starting on page 191 will help you deal with some of the most common questions that young people may ask about Christianity in general, and about Mark's Gospel in particular.

PRAY

- that those invited will attend the course.
- that God would enable you to prepare well.
- for the logistics of organizing the course.
- for good relationships with your co-leaders and young people.
- that God would equip you to lead faithfully.
- that the Holy Spirit would open the blind eyes of those who attend.
- *Take time now to pray through the points above.*

During the course...

It's worthwhile understanding the reasons why we have structured the course the way we have. At first sight some of the things we suggest might seem irrelevant, but can we urge you to run the programme as we have developed it before you start to adapt it?

FOOD

Eating together is an important part of each week at CY as it helps people to get to know each other and feel comfortable in the group. But you don't have to be sitting formally at a table for the meal to work well! Teenagers and students are often happier to eat "on the go". Although there may be a good reason to do something more formal at some stage.

Take the lead in introducing people to each other. Try to avoid theological discussions during this time. The intention is to share life, and allow people to relax and get used to the environment and the other people – not to be spiritually intense.

The mealtime is not an opportunity to buttonhole individuals, although if an opportunity arises naturally for you to talk about your faith, you should take it.

GROUP ACTIVITY

The activities are designed to tie into the theme of each week. It is important that they do not dominate but are integrated into everything else in the course. Often you will not need to make a conscious link between the activity and what follows, but some suggestions are given in the guide for how you could do this.

Make sure everyone is involved in the activity – including you!

EXPLORE

EXPLORE is a short Bible study from Mark's Gospel. [See page 44 for an example.]

Sit where you can see everyone. That way, you can make eye contact with people, and it also ensures that they can see you too. It's not a good idea for leaders to sit next to one another, as it can look intimidating.

Because the theme of the group activity is designed to tie in with EXPLORE, try to refer to what was learned during the activity.

During EXPLORE, your responsibility as a leader is more than just asking the Bible study questions. You should try to maintain a relaxed atmosphere and involve everyone in the discussion if possible. Try to avoid using Christian jargon that might confuse your group. And don't forget how important the tone of your voice and your body language can be as you lead the study.

It's important to listen carefully to the answers given by participants and to reply graciously. Young people need to know that they are valued and that their opinions are important to you.

Encourage your young people to write down the answers in the space provided in their Handbook. If they write things down, they are more likely to remember them, and the act of writing reinforces the message.

Sample answers are provided for you in this book, although it is vital to prepare for EXPLORE by reading and thinking through the questions yourself in advance.

If you are asked a question that you don't know the answer to, **don't panic.** Offer to think about the question, do some research, and get back to the person next week. Write the question down and seek help from a good book or another leader. See www. christianityexplored.org/reading for recommended reading. There are sample answers in this book to questions on Mark (page 197) and on more general questions (page 203).

You should be able to complete the study in 15 minutes at a run, but if you have longer then this can be 25 minutes. If you are behind schedule, don't feel you have to rush through the questions. If participants are stuck on some aspect of the Bible study, either from Mark or from somewhere else, feel free to discuss these things instead, if the group is interested. You can always finish the study during the TALKBACK section, after the talk or DVD, if you like.

TALK/DVD
After EXPLORE, a talk is presented or the *Soul* DVD is shown. After you've heard the talks or watched the DVD a few times, it can be tempting to listen less attentively! But be aware that the group is likely to follow your lead, and stop listening too.

TALKBACK
TALKBACK is an opportunity to respond to the issues raised during the talk/DVD. Use the questions provided to help your group unpack the truths that have been presented.

Again, it is not important to finish all the questions. They are just an aid to discussion. There are some additional questions added to the leader's material in this book if your group is able and willing to spend more time discussing things. Add your own supplementary questions as necessary to ensure that participants have grasped the issues. There will be a tendency with most groups to drift away from discussing the Bible in particular into general questions and ideas. It is your job as group leader to **always** try to direct attention back to the Bible.

As with EXPLORE, the aim is to allow young people to discover Christ through Mark's Gospel; to encourage and guide discussion, rather than to lecture. As a general rule, they should be talking more than you are!

Encourage the group to ask questions and thank people when they ask helpful questions about a subject. This will promote discussion and openness in the groups.

Listen carefully to all questions and answers. They will give you a good indication of each person's understanding and spiritual maturity. A wrong answer will often reveal as much, if not more than, a right answer. And a question that is "off-topic" can expose the most pressing issue in a person's life.

Bear in mind that the questions participants raise may subtly indicate more fundamental objections to Christianity. For instance, if someone seems to have a problem believing that Jonah could have survived in a giant fish for three days, trying to give detailed examples of the regurgitation of human beings by large aquatic creatures is probably unwise. It would be better to see that the participant's real issue is most likely the general trustworthiness of the Bible, and deal with that.

Many questions in TALKBACK have personal applications. Depending on your group, participants may feel shy about answering these in front of others. Giving your own answer can encourage them to do so. Otherwise, feel free to ask participants to answer questions in their own Handbook rather than out loud.

ENDING THE SESSION

Always finish at the promised time. Good timekeeping develops trust in the group, and with their parents!

Let participants know that they are welcome to stay and talk further if they like. Time spent talking with young people after the study officially ends gives you a great opportunity to find out where individuals are in their understanding of the gospel.

Seek to explain what they have not understood. Encourage them by sharing your own testimony if appropriate. Help them to see the need for a personal response to Jesus Christ, but do not pressure them.

In other editions of *Christianity Explored*, participants are encouraged to complete a "Home Study", which consists of a series of questions on a passage or a reading from Mark's Gospel. In developing CY, we found that young people tended to view Home Study as homework and so it was rarely done. As a result, we recommend that you simply encourage your young people to read Mark's Gospel through the course. Copies of Mark's Gospel themed for CY are available, and a reading plan is contained in the back of their Handbook, entitled "The Mark Challenge". Don't refer to it as home study – just make it clear that reading Mark will help them to get the most out of CY.

THE MARK CHALLENGE

At the back of the *CY* and *CY Nano Handbooks* is a page called "The Mark Challenge". It's basically a reading plan which will take someone through the whole of the Gospel of Mark in three weeks. As well as looking in detail at smaller sections of Mark in the CY sessions, you may want to encourage your group to pick up *The Mark Challenge* to read right the way through the Gospel during the time they are doing CY. This will help them get hold of the sweep of the Gospel story, and to see the parts they are looking at in more detail in the context of the whole book.

It is quite common for people never to have read through a whole Gospel, even if they are familiar with some stories in it. It is quite common for people to have formed an opinion about Jesus when they have never read a complete Gospel!

If you have issued *The Mark Challenge* it may therefore be appropriate to include some time during the session to ask people to feed back questions, thoughts or comments on what they have been reading in Mark throughout the week.

Some things to consider:

- **Don't make it sound like homework!** Present it as a challenge to them to read the whole book.

- **Do give them some opportunity to feed back on what they have read,** and a place to ask their questions – detailed notes on issues that may arise from their reading can be found on page 197.

- **Be careful** that any discussion at the CY sessions does not turn into "Bible-study overkill". The ones who have done The Mark Challenge may be keen to talk. The ones who have not will not know what is being talked about, and may easily get bored – especially if the discussion drags on or gets technical. It could be an opportunity to offer to discuss privately any questions with those who have taken up the challenge.

- If they are able to get into the habit of daily Bible reading during CY, then be prepared to offer them something else to keep them going afterwards. *Discover*, *Engage*, *Explore*, or *Start* from The Good Book Company are good options, depending on the age of the group.

Identity, Mission and Call in Mark's Gospel

As a leader preparing to teach Mark, there's no substitute for reading through Mark's Gospel at least two or three times. And as you read, you'll begin to see that Mark is preoccupied with three great themes:

- Who is Jesus? (Jesus' identity)
- Why did he come? (Jesus' mission)
- What does he demand? (Jesus' call)

Every passage in Mark has something to say to us about one or more of those themes.

Broadly speaking, the first half of Mark (1:1 – 8:30) is taken up with the question of Jesus' identity: it starts by saying, "The beginning of the gospel about Jesus Christ, the Son of God" and ends with Peter's statement, "You are the Christ."

The second half of Mark's Gospel is largely taken up with the question of Jesus' mission, which is why it is so dominated by the cross. By way of example, look at one of the most significant passages in Mark's Gospel – Mark chapter 8, verses 27 to 38 – and you'll discover all three themes (identity, mission and call) in quick succession. Let's take a few verses at a time.

IDENTITY

The dominant question in **verses 27–30** is Jesus' identity. Who exactly is Jesus?

> "Jesus and his disciples went on to the villages around Caesarea Philippi. On the way he asked them, 'Who do people say I am?' They replied, 'Some say John the Baptist; others say Elijah; and still others, one of the prophets.' 'But what about you?' he asked. 'Who do you say I am?' Peter answered, 'You are the Christ.' Jesus warned them not to tell anyone about him."

People had lots of theories about Jesus' identity, just as they do now: "Some say John the Baptist; others say Elijah; and still others, one of the prophets."

But Jesus gets very personal in verse 29: "What about you? … Who do you say I am?"

Peter answers the question about Jesus' identity correctly: "You are the Christ." Jesus is not "one of the prophets" as some were saying. He is actually the Christ – the fulfilment of all prophecy.

But although Peter has Jesus' identity right, it's clear he hasn't yet understood Jesus' mission.

MISSION

Let's look at **Mark 8:31–33** to discover Jesus' mission.

> "He then began to teach them that the Son of Man must suffer many things and be rejected by the elders, chief priests and teachers of the law, and that he must be killed and after three days rise again. He spoke plainly about this, and Peter took him aside and began to rebuke him. But when Jesus turned and looked at his disciples, he rebuked Peter. 'Get behind me, Satan!' he said. 'You do not have in mind the things of God, but the things of men.'"

Here, for the first time, Jesus begins to teach them his mission – that he "must suffer many things and be rejected by the elders, chief priests and teachers of the law, and that he must be killed and after three days rise again".

Jesus doesn't leave any room for misunderstanding (he "spoke plainly about this") because he knows that the disciples – and most of the public – have a very different expectation of what the Christ would be like. He would be a triumphant king, marching in to claim his territory, trampling the enemy underfoot and ushering in a glorious new era for his followers. A Christ who suffered and died would have seemed like a contradiction in terms.

Peter clearly has this triumphal view of the Christ in mind when he takes Jesus aside and begins "to rebuke him". But Jesus' strong reaction shows just how necessary death is to his mission: "Get behind me, Satan! … You do not have in mind the things of God, but the things of men." The idea that the so-called "Son of God" had to suffer and die is still a stumbling block for many people today. But if we're to understand Mark's Gospel – and indeed the whole Bible – correctly, it is essential to grasp the true nature of Jesus' mission: he "must suffer" and "he must be killed" so that we can be forgiven.

If that is Jesus' identity and mission, what are the implications for his followers?

CALL

What is Christ's call? Let's look at **Mark 8:34.**

> "Then he called the crowd to him along with his disciples and said: 'If anyone would come after me, he must deny himself and take up his cross and follow me.'"

Having just spoken to the disciples about his own death, he calls the crowd to him and says, "If anyone would come after me, he must deny himself and take up his cross and follow me." It is striking, and not a little disturbing, to see Jesus immediately turn his attention from the cross he must take up to the cross *we* must take up.

First, if we are to follow him, Jesus tells us we must deny ourselves. It is not a natural thing for human beings to turn away from their natural self-centeredness and self-reliance, but that is Jesus' call. We cannot follow him unless we deny our own selfish instincts.

Second, we cannot follow Jesus if we are not prepared to take up our cross. We must be prepared to serve him – and others – to the point of giving up our lives. In effect, Jesus must be more important to us than life itself.

If that seems irrational, we need to hear what Jesus says next in **verses 35–38:**

> *"For whoever wants to save his life will lose it, but whoever loses his life for me and for the gospel will save it. What good is it for a man to gain the whole world, yet forfeit his soul? Or what can a man give in exchange for his soul? If anyone is ashamed of me and my words in this adulterous and sinful generation, the Son of Man will be ashamed of him when he comes in his Father's glory with the holy angels."*

The first reason to obey Christ's call is in verse 35: if we give up our life for him, we'll save it; and if we don't, we'll lose it. That's the amazing thing about Jesus – you give him your life, and you find it. People today are always talking about "finding themselves". Jesus is the answer to that quest.

Second, verse 36 says that even if we were to gain the whole world by rejecting Jesus, we would still lose the most important thing we have – our soul. That's a great reason for obeying Christ's call. What is the most important thing to us? Our college education, our career, our boyfriend/girlfriend, our family? Or is it our soul – our true, real inner life?

The third reason to obey Jesus' call is in verse 37. If we miss out on eternal life, there is nothing we can do to buy it back. No wealth we may have accumulated, no worldly popularity, no friends in high places can win back the soul we will lose by not obeying Jesus' call.

And the fourth reason Jesus gives for obeying his call is in verse 38. If we reject Jesus, then he will reject us when he returns as judge of the world. So if the future belongs to Jesus, then it makes perfect sense to give him our time, our resources, our lives, and our love.

So that's Jesus' identity, mission and call in Mark 8.

IDENTITY	**MISSION**	**CALL**
Who is Jesus?	*Why did Jesus come?*	*What does Jesus demand?*
MARK 8:27-30	**MARK 8:31-33**	**MARK 8:34-38**

EXERCISE: *Read through the whole of Mark's Gospel and decide whether each paragraph is about Jesus' identity, mission or call. Label each one "I", "M", or "C", remembering that some paragraphs may be a combination of two or three of the above.*

What to do if...

... THERE'S SILENCE!

If a question is met with silence, don't be too quick to speak. Allow people time to think. They might be considering how to phrase their answer, or they could just be shy about speaking first. One of the following techniques might be useful:

- If you sense that someone knows the answer but is shy about giving it, ask them by name. Often they will be happy to be asked.

- It might be appropriate to try a "game" – asking them to raise their hand if they agree or disagree with certain answers as you give them.

- It may help to divide people into groups of two or three to work through questions and then have them feed their answers back to the whole group.

- You might also try offering some help with finding the answers; for example, you might say, "There's a clue at the end of verse 2".

... ONE PERSON ANSWERS ALL THE QUESTIONS

- Thank them for their answers. Try asking the group: "What do other people think?"

- Direct a few questions at the other participants by name.

- Sit *beside* the talkative participant the following week. That will make it harder for them to catch your eye and answer the questions.

- If the situation continues, you may need to say something to the participant after the study and ask them to give others an opportunity to answer next time. For example: *"Thank you so much for everything you are contributing. I wonder if you could help me with the quieter people in the group..."*

... SOMEONE GIVES THE WRONG ANSWER

- **Do not immediately correct them.** Give the person the opportunity to correct themselves. Ask them, for example: *"What does verse 4 tell us about that?"* If they are still unable to answer correctly, give others the chance (for example: *"Does anyone disagree or want to add anything?"*).

- **Graciously correct.** If necessary, don't be afraid graciously to correct a wrong answer that may mislead others. Say something like: *"Thank you, that's an interesting point, but I'm not sure that's quite what's going on here."*

- Have further questions in mind to develop the initial answer. For example: *"What did you mean by that?"* or *"What does everyone else think?"* or *"Where does it say that?"* If no one is able to answer the question, give the correct answer, showing from the Bible passage why it is the right answer.

...PEOPLE DO NOT ENGAGE WITH THE DISCUSSION

This is a common problem when working with young people. Try making eye contact with the person to get them involved again with the discussion.

- You could try using an illustration or a story which relates to the subject of your discussion, as this will often draw people back in.

- If you know the person reasonably well, you could try asking a direct question to encourage them to participate.

- Sometimes, people just don't want to engage that week. This will often change the following week. If the suggestions above don't work, focus on those who are interested in the discussion, making the most of the time with the participants who want to listen and engage.

...SOMEONE ASKS A DISTRACTING QUESTION

A question may be raised that does not relate to the study and will take the group off track. Offer to discuss the issue later with the person.

... SOMEONE ASKS ME A QUESTION I CANNOT ANSWER

Lead honestly. You won't be able to answer every question. Some questions can be easily addressed, but others will be difficult. If you don't know the answer, say so – but tell them that you'll try to have an answer ready for the following week.

- **Lend them a book.** It may be best to give them a suitable book to help them. See www.christianityexplored.org/reading for suggestions.

...SOMEONE IS DISRUPTIVE

If someone is being disruptive, try first of all to get them back into the discussion. It might be necessary to talk to them later about why they are being disruptive. Often this is because they are frustrated by the content, or upset by the group they're in. Sometimes, "reassigning" the person to one of the other groups can turn a disruptive participant into an active one.

Deliberately stupid or silly answers can also be a disruptive influence. If it is appropriate, laugh with the group, then gently try to bring the discussion back on track. If the comments are inappropriate or repeated, speak with the person afterwards and ask them to hold back their comments during discussions.

...SOMEONE DOES NOT WANT TO DO THE ACTIVITIES

Show enthusiasm and enjoyment yourself. This will encourage others to take part in the activities. Usually, non-interaction will change as people get to know you and the group, and begin to see that the activities are being enjoyed by everyone else.

... PARTICIPANTS DON'T COME BACK

If you've already established a good relationship with that person, contact him or her once to say you missed them and that it would be great to see them next time, but don't put pressure on them.

... PARTICIPANTS MISS ONE SESSION OR MORE

Welcome them back and during the meal try and summarise what they have missed. Encourage them to read the passages in Mark they have missed and to work through the questions in the Handbook as their daily reading. Let them know that they can come back to you with anything they are concerned about or do not understand.

... A PASTORAL ISSUE EMERGES THAT I AM NOT QUALIFIED TO DEAL WITH

- Do not to try and deal with the situation if you feel you are out of your depth. Encourage the person to go with you to see your pastor or a Christian counsellor.

- Check your church's child protection policy and make sure that you understand what your obligations and responsibilities are if the young person you are dealing with reveals that they are in any kind of danger.

- Offer to pray with them, or for them about the issue, if that is appropriate.

- Do not break a confidence without asking their permission first. However, in extreme circumstances you may need to do so even if they refuse to give you permission.

FEEDBACK FORM EXAMPLE

You can download printer-friendly versions of this form in various sizes and designs from **www.christianityexplored.org/cy**

Name

1 Before you began CY, how would you have described yourself?

☐ I didn't believe in God

☐ I wasn't sure if God existed or not

☐ I believed in God but not in Jesus Christ

☐ A Christian

☐ Something else _____

2 Now that you've finished CY, how would you describe yourself?

☐ I understand who Jesus is, why he came and what it means to follow him. I have put my trust in him.

☐ I wouldn't call myself a Christian, but I would like to find out more.

☐ Other _____

3 If you have not yet put your trust in Jesus, what is stopping you?

4 What would you like to do now?

☐ I am interested in joining a follow-up course (a course that will help me to continue in the Christian life).

☐ I'd like to read the Christianity Explored book to help me remember what I discovered.

☐ I don't want to do anything more at this stage.

☐ I would like to join a church.

☐ I am happy at the church I go to.

5 On a scale of 1 to 10 how much did you enjoy CY?
(1 = I really hated it; 10 = I really loved it.)

6 Anything else you'd like to tell us?

After the course...

Jesus warns us in the Parable of the Sower (Mark 4:3–20) that there will be a variety of responses to the preaching of the gospel. It is worth thinking in advance about what you will do for the following responses:

- *What will you do for those for whom the message has "gone in one ear and out the other"?*

- *How will you help the shallow enthusiasts to deepen their response?*

- *How will you provide a support for those who are vulnerable to having their initial commitment squeezed out of them by the pressure of their families, friends or their own personal ambitions?*

- *And how will you help young disciples to continue growing in their understanding, godliness and love?*

It's vital to have a follow-up strategy in place for all your young people.

GIVE OUT FEEDBACK FORMS
Feedback forms, given out during the last week of the course, are a great way to challenge your young people to think about where they currently are with Christ, and to help leaders plan a way forward once the course is ended. See opposite for an example feedback form.

STAY IN TOUCH
CY is not a conveyor belt that either ships young people into the Christian faith – or tips them off into the street outside. Having spent seven sessions with your group considering profound and personal issues, you will know them well – and they will know you well.

Under these circumstances, it would clearly be wrong to "drop" participants once the course comes to an end. Plan to stay in touch with all the people in your group, and arrange with your co-leaders that each person has at least one Christian who remains in touch with him or her.

If your CY group is largely comprised of regular group members, then staying in touch should be less difficult. For people who have yet to make up their minds about the Christian faith, encourage them to continue thinking through the basics in the context of the regular group meetings. Never, ever close the door to them.

ARRANGE FOLLOW-UP

There is an opportunity at the end of the course for participants to express their commitment to Christ with a prayer. But be wary of thinking that this is the end of your role. Jesus calls us not to get people to "pray the prayer", but to "make disciples" (Matthew 28:19).

If anyone in your group has made a commitment to Christ, help them lay firm foundations so that they will be able to persevere. Make sure that they get involved in some form of regular Bible study and some area of Christian service.

You should invite them to start coming along to church if they're not already attending regularly. It's a great idea to encourage them to meet with others beforehand and go as a group.

PRAY

A supremely Christ-like way of caring for people is to pray for them. Even after the course has ended, it is important to pray for all the members of the group.

For new believers, pray for growth, fruitfulness and joy. For those who have not yet made a commitment, pray that the Lord will have mercy on them and send his Holy Spirit to open their blind eyes.

Pray for yourself, for patience and wisdom as you wait for God's word to do its work.

PLAN THE NEXT CY COURSE!

Evangelism should be part of the DNA of the way you run your group. Many people run CY once, and then think they have "done" their evangelism for the next few years.

And your existing group members will be the ones who will be your natural "bringers" for a new course. Make sure that you plan to run the course while their memory of it is still strong and their enthusiasm to invite others is high.

To add variety, so that those who have previously been on a CY course do not get bored or apathetic, you could change the venue, timing or leaders. You could also vary the activities and illustrations you use. Or you could switch between using the DVDs and doing the talks "live", or vice versa.

CY Nano
Study Guide

Before we begin

This section contains the studies to work through over the seven-week *CY Nano* course. It includes all the material in the group member's *CY Nano Handbook*, together with a range of activities, and answers to the questions.

The *CY Nano* course has been designed with 11-14s in mind. The talks have been written for this age group, and the activities and questions are designed to be accessible and enjoyable for young teenagers.

However, you know your group best. It may be appropriate to choose some activities from the older *CY* course, which can be found in Section 3 of this Leader's Guide. You may also decide that replacing some or all of the talks with episodes from the *Soul DVD* will suit your particular group better. We have aimed to keep the material as flexible as possible to allow you to make these adjustments easily if they would help your group.

Note: In the notes that follow, the **bold text** shown in the light grey boxes (like this one) is the material that appears in the CY Nano Handbook used by group members.

CY it's worth exploring

▶ *Welcome the group and thank them for coming. Introduce yourself if necessary, letting them know that you are there to help and answer any questions they might have.*

▶ *Explain how the session will work and what time it will finish. Let the group know what kinds of things they will be doing, eg:* We'll be doing some warm-up activities to get to know each other a little, having a brief discussion, listening to a talk, and then looking together at a bit of the Bible. There will be plenty of time and opportunity for you to ask any question you want to.

▶ *Explain that no one will be asked to read out loud, pray, or answer any question they don't want to.*

OPTIONAL GROUP ACTIVITY

▶ *If you have time, start the session with one of the following icebreaker activities. You may also want to look at the activities suggested for the older age group, 2-MINUTE MIXER and TRUE OR FALSE on pages 115-116, as they may suit your group.*

SIGNATURE BINGO

Aim: To get everyone to know each other and to "break the ice".

Equipment: Bingo sheet for each member of the group (either download this sheet from www.christianityexplored.org/cy or make your own from sheets of paper divided into nine squares); pens; small bag; small strips of paper; two small prizes for winners; a CD/MP3 player (optional).

- ❂ Give every participant a strip of paper and a pen. Ask them to write their own name on the paper and put it in the bag.

- ❂ Next, give every participant a piece of paper divided into nine squares.

- ❂ Ask them to fill their grid with signatures from other people, putting one signature in each of the nine squares. If appropriate, play music in the background – you could fit this part of the activity to the length of one particular song track – make sure it's only about 3 minutes long to add some urgency to the task.

Leader's checklist

Have you...

☐ Made it clear to people the time and place where you will meet?

☐ Collected any items needed for the activities?

☐ Enough Bibles or Mark's Gospels for the group?

☐ CY Nano Handbooks and a pen or pencil for each group member?

☐ Prepared the talk and added any personal illustrations? (Or set up the optional Soul DVD if using it.)

☐ Thought through your answers to each of the questions?

☐ Prayed for each group member and yourself as the leader?

- Tell the group that you are going to play bingo with their names, and that a prize will be awarded for the first completed line and the first completed card.

- Take one name out of the bag at a time. As you call out someone's name, ask them to say "hello" (and maybe tell the group one piece of information about him/herself). If someone has this name on their card they can cross it out. Once someone has a line they can call "bingo".

- Have a prize ready for the first completed line and first completed card.

Note: If the group is too large, play this game in table groups, rather than with the whole group – and tell your leaders beforehand so that they are ready to lead a table each.

HOT POTATO

Aim: To get everyone to know each other and to "break the ice".

Equipment: One or more potatoes, depending on the size of your group; a CD/MP3 player; a list of actions (eg: cluck like a chicken, whistle the first line of "Happy Birthday", pat your head while rubbing your tummy, spell your name backwards…)

- Divide into groups of five or more - then ask each group to sit in a circle.

- Give each group a potato.

- When the music starts, each group passes the potato round the circle.

- Whoever is holding the potato when the music stops has to stand up, say their name, and then perform the action you give them (eg: turn around three times). They then sit down again and, when the music starts, pass the potato on.

- From then on, every time that person gets the potato they have to stand up, say their name and perform their action before passing the potato on.

- Keep playing, with a new person being given an action each time, until the whole group are doing actions while passing the potato along.

EXPLORE

▶ *Hand a CY Nano Handbook to each participant. Ask them to turn to page 4 and to write down their answer to this question:*

> **If you could ask God one question, and you knew it would be answered, what would it be?**

▶ *Ask the group to share their answers. Note down what they are so that you can deal with them at some point during the course. Don't attempt to answer all the questions at this time, but do acknowledge every question and assure participants that they will be covered during CY Nano. (Some questions will be answered by the talks and some – like questions about suffering – are best dealt with after the talks on the cross / grace.) However, you may want to answer one or two short questions at this point, if they are simple to deal with and not contentious. You might also want to write your own question and share it with the group. Note: If your group members would be embarrassed to say their questions, ask them to write them on a piece of paper and put them in a "question box".* You can then collect all the questions from the box and read them to the group.

▶ *Either here, or after the talk, the group may ask questions on science/evolution/ creation. Make sure you plan a time to talk about this – probably during a later session, using the notes on page 206. It may be enough at this point to say that the course is not making any particular point about evolution or creation. We're simply showing that we are either the result of an accident or we have been made by someone – and that this makes a difference to how we see "the meaning of life".*

GROUP ACTIVITY : POSTER

▶ *Give the group one large piece of paper and some pens. Ask them to draw a poster of things that come into their minds when they think of Christianity. For example, they might draw a large cathedral or church. If some of the group prefer not to draw, they can write single words on the poster instead.*

Note: *Leaders need to allow the group to draw what they want. If they want to draw something that is theologically problematic, allow them to do it because there will be an opportunity later to correct misunderstandings.*

▶ *Give each person a Bible. Show them where they can find Mark's Gospel. Explain how chapters and verses work.*

▶ *Ask everyone to turn to* **Mark 1:1**. *(***Note:*** *The questions and quotes in CY Nano are based on the NIV.)*

▶ *One of the leaders should read* **Mark 1:1** *aloud; then the group should work through the questions below. The answers are given here for your reference.*

What does Mark say Christianity is all about in the first sentence of his book?

● He says that it is "good news". (Explain that the word "gospel" means "good news".)

● He says it's about Jesus.

● He says it's about Jesus being the Son of God. (*see note on this below)

*Note: *Some eagle-eyed participants may notice a footnote in the NIV that says: "Some ancient manuscripts do not have the words 'the Son of God'", and ask you about it. This may, in turn, raise all kinds of issues about the reliability of the Bible, and the trustworthiness of Mark. If this is an issue for your group, or for an individual, plan to include some input on the reliability of the Bible. See notes on page 203.*

How is that different from some of the pictures we've drawn?

This question is designed to tackle some of the common misconceptions about the Christian faith that may have come up in the poster-drawing exercise.

● He says that it is "good news". In other words – it's not bad news; it's great, brilliant and exciting news – far from boring! If you think Christianity is boring, then you've not really understood what it's all about.

- He says it's about Jesus. It's not about buildings, or services, or "religion" – it's about a man who lived and walked and breathed in history, called Jesus.

- He says it's about Jesus being the Son of God. It's about God making himself known to us through Jesus.

TALK 1

▶ *Deliver Talk 1 using the notes below. The notes for this talk can also be downloaded from www.christianityexplored.org/cy to enable you to adapt them for your group and add your own illustrations. Alternatively, you could show Episode 1 from the Soul DVD if this would be appropriate for your group.*

▶ *There is a recap (called DOWNLOAD) in the participant's CY Nano Handbook for their reference. Encourage people to write notes on the Download page as they listen to the talk.*

OUTLINE OF TALK ONE: CY IT'S WORTH EXPLORING

▶ *Use the outline below to develop your own talk. This outline can also be downloaded from www.christianityexplored.org/cy.*

Aim

- To welcome people to the course.

- To make the point that many people have the wrong impression of Christianity.

- To explain that Christianity is not about rules or ceremonies. It's all about Jesus Christ.

- To explain that we can only find true significance and real meaning in our lives once we realize that there's a God who created us and who wants us to know him.

- To explain that we can only get to know God through Jesus, and that we're going to find out about him during CY.

Introductory illustration

▶ *Tell the group a funny/interesting example of what you used to think about Christianity. Use a personal example if you can, but if you don't have one (perhaps because you have been a Christian from a young age), interview another leader or talk about someone you know. Keep the illustration short. Alternatively, show a short clip from a film (eg: Mr Bean in church) or cartoon (eg: The Simpsons in church) – check that you can do this legally.*

Opening

- Loads of people have different ideas about Christianity. It often depends on whether they know any Christians, or have had experience of being in a church.

- Your poster lists some of those ideas.

▶ *Talk about some of the pictures drawn on the poster. Be careful not to make any negative comments – the aim is just to discover the range of ideas your group members currently have. There will be opportunity later in the course to discuss some of these views, so do keep the poster, or make a note of what was drawn, so that you can be sure to address these issues at some point.*

1. What is Christianity about?

- Many people think that Christianity is about religious ceremonies, or keeping a set of rules. Mark says something very different from that. As we saw in the very first sentence of Mark's book, Christianity is all about a person, Jesus Christ.

▶ *Explain that the Bibles you're using have extra bits added to help you find the section you want. These extras include the chapter and verse numbers, and also the headings. So Mark didn't write the heading above verse 1 – the publishers added it.*

- Mark's own heading is really verse 1, where he tells us exactly what his book is about.

▶ *Read **Mark 1:1** aloud.*

- Mark's entire book is about:

    - a man called **Jesus**

    - whose title is the "**Christ**" (which means "God's chosen King")

    - who is the **Son of God**.

- The rest of Mark's book shows us what these things mean, and why he believes they are true. So as we do *CY Nano* together, we will be looking at Jesus Christ and finding out what Mark tells us about him.

- We'll also be thinking about some of the big questions people ask about life – questions like "Where did life come from?" and "What's the purpose of life?"

2. Where did life come from?

▶ *You may want to include a funny illustration here – maybe display a cartoon picture about where life came from. Alternatively, show or read out the following: "one bucket of water, eight bars of soap, one nail and the head of a matchstick". Ask your group if they know what this makes? (Answer: these sum up the chemical contents of a human body!)*

- Scientists spend billions every year trying to work out exactly how the earth began and where life came from. You've probably learned about some of their ideas in school or from books and television programmes.

- There are two possible answers to this question. Either we are here by chance, or someone made us.

- If we are here by chance, it means we have no real significance or value. We're just a bunch of chemicals who wander around the earth meeting other bunches of chemicals. We have no value; we don't matter; because we're just a splodge of atoms in a body!

- If we have been made by someone, if we have been created, that makes a huge difference. The Bible says that God created us, that we are his workmanship. This means that we matter enormously. God says so.

- We don't matter because of having the best gadgets or wearing the latest fashion. We don't matter because of where we come from or what we're good at. Instead, we matter – and matter enormously – because God created us. He made us, he loves us, and he has a purpose for our lives. Our lives mean something.

3. What's the point of life?

- ● Where life comes from makes a huge difference when we start thinking about death. Most people don't like talking about death, even though every one of us will face death sooner or later. But since we all have to die, what's the point of living?

- ● Lots of people have tried to work out what the point of life is. If we had drawn a poster about that, I'm sure we would have come up with loads of different ideas. TV, magazines and the internet often give the impression that the answer is to be rich, famous and good looking. But they're also quick to tell us stories of celebrities who haven't found happiness as a result.

■ *Include an illustration here of someone who has been in the news recently because their success has left them depressed, suicidal or turning to drugs or alcohol.*

- ● You would think that fame and money would lead to happiness, but plenty of celebrities find that it doesn't. So they turn to drugs, drinking or even suicide. Why?

- ● Well, the Bible says that we don't really start living until we know the one who made us, and live as he made us to live. So the question is, how can we know God?

4. Getting to know God

■ *Choose a popular celebrity for this illustration. What would you do if you really wanted to get to know _____ ? (Fill in the name of a suitable celebrity for your group.) Maybe you could go to where they live and call out their name as they leave the house. Or you could try to find their phone number, email or Twitter address. But they probably wouldn't reply. The only way you're going to be able to get to know _____ is if they want to know you. It would have to be him/her who contacted you and arranged to meet up.*

- ● The same is true if we want to know the one who made us. People have tried knowing God by thinking deeply about him, or using their imagination to find out what he's like, but we can't get to know God that way. We can't get to know God by ourselves at all.

- ● We need God to reveal himself to us. Mark says that God has done that by sending Jesus Christ. That's why Mark's book is all about Jesus. If we want to know what God is like, we must look at Jesus.

Conclusion

- ● There's a word in Mark's first sentence that tells us why looking at Jesus is such a good idea. The word is "gospel", and it means "good news". The news about Jesus isn't bad or boring – it's good news.

- ● During *CY Nano* we're going to explore what Mark tells us about who Jesus is, and about why he came. We're also going to think about what it means to live as a Christian – what it means to follow Jesus.

- ● So is this course worth sticking with for seven weeks? The reason I think you'll find it's worth doing is because Jesus is the only way we can know the one who made us and understand the point of life. Jesus answers those big questions we've been thinking about: "Where did life come from?" and "What's the point of living?"

- ● That's why "the gospel about Jesus Christ" is good news.

DOWNLOAD

The recap below (called DOWNLOAD) appears in the participant's CY Nano Handbook for their reference.

- ◉ Christianity is not about rules or ceremonies. It's all about Jesus Christ.

- ◉ If we're here by chance, we don't matter or have any value. But God created us - so we matter enormously.

- ◉ We all face death sooner or later. Since we all have to die, what's the point of living?

- ◉ The Bible says we don't really start living until we know the one who made us, and live as he made us to live.

- ◉ But how can we get to know God? We need him to show himself to us. Mark says he's done that for us by sending Jesus Christ. If we want to know what God's like, we must look at Jesus.

- ◉ That's why "the gospel about Jesus Christ" is good news.

TALKBACK

▶ *Use the questions below to encourage discussion (they are also printed in the participant's CY Nano Handbook).*

▶ *Remember that this is the first session, and the aim here is not to explain the whole gospel, to challenge them to become Christians, or start an argument about what they currently believe. It is simply to open up the themes that will be covered in subsequent weeks.*

▶ *Be careful that TALKBACK does not run over time. It is much better to stop a good discussion, leaving them hungry for more, than to talk everything out in detail with the risk of boring some of the group, or putting them off coming back next time.*

> **If you asked a group of people in the street: "What's the point of life?", what kind of answers would you get?**

- ◉ Answers might include: making lots of money; having a good time; having good friends; finding love.

- ◉ You might ask your group why they think different people would give different answers to this question.

- ◉ The aim here is not to criticize these views, but to get the group thinking about the meaning of life. There is no pressing need to comment on them now, unless the discussion naturally heads that way.

What do most people think about God and Christianity? ✔ **your answers**

boring	**full of rules**	**interesting**
pointless	**important**	**same as other religions**
out of date	**only for Sundays**	add your own suggestion here

Why do you think that is?

- ❯ This is to recap the EXPLORE questions, without getting too personal. Answers may include: boring, irrelevant, outdated, full of rules etc.

- ❯ Explain that churches can very easily forget that Christianity is all about Jesus – and the resulting religion can become any or all of those things. But this is not real Christianity.

- ❯ If necessary, sympathize with anyone in the group who may have had a bad experience of religion – an unhelpful minister, boring services etc.

What about Jesus? Do people think he matters? What do *you* think?

- ❯ At this stage don't press anyone to give an answer for what they think, but if they do, it may be appropriate to ask them why.

- ❯ Remind them that, according to Mark 1:1, Jesus is "good news".

CONCLUSION

Finish by encouraging your group members to come back next time. Tell them: We've seen that Mark says that Christianity is all about one man, Jesus. Next week we'll find out about some of the things Jesus did and said, and why Mark says that Jesus is "good news".

AFTERWARDS

- ❯ Write down the questions that people have come up with, so that you can be sure to address them in the coming weeks. It may be helpful at this point to prepare a plan of which question you deal with each session.

- ❯ Think about the people who came. Make a list so that you can pray for them.

- ❯ Think about what contact you may want to make during the week to encourage them to come the next time.

CY Jesus matters

▶ *Welcome the group and thank them for coming.*

▶ *Recap on the previous week:*
Last time we saw that Christianity is not about beautiful buildings and boring services – it is all about Jesus Christ.
Remember Mark chapter 1, verse 1? "The beginning of the gospel about Jesus Christ, the Son of God."
But what was Jesus really like? Well, that's what we're going to look at this time.

GROUP ACTIVITY
▶ *Choose one of the following activities, to suit your group and the time you have available.*

GUESS WHO?
Aim: To show that a person's qualities reveal their true identity.

Equipment: Powerpoint projector; slide show which you can make yourself or download from www.christianityexplored.org/cy; a prize. (Alternatively, if you don't have access to a projector, you can simply read the clues out loud.)

- Each powerpoint slide contains five pieces of information (clues) about famous people. Choose both positive and negative examples of famous people. The clues are revealed one by one.

- Each team has to try and guess who is being described on the slide.

- The teams score according to how soon they guess correctly:

  - After clue 1   10 points
  - After clue 2   8 points
  - After clue 3   6 points
  - After clue 4   4 points
  - After clue 5   2 points

- The team with the most points wins the prize.

For Small Groups: Play with two teams and allow each team to guess once after each clue. The team who guesses correctly then gains the

---

Leader's checklist

Have you...

- ☐ Reminded group members where and when you will meet (eg: by email or text message)?

- ☐ Collected any items needed for the activities?

- ☐ Enough Bibles or Mark's Gospels for the group?

- ☐ CY Nano Handbooks and a pen or pencil for each group member?

- ☐ Prepared the talk and added any personal illustrations? (Or set up the optional Soul DVD if using it.)

- ☐ Thought through your answers to each of the questions?

- ☐ Prayed for each group member and yourself as the leader?

points. (Even after a team guesses correctly, you should still display the remaining clues and read them out loud.)

For Larger Groups: Give each table group leader the identities of the people on each slide so that they can score for their team. (This is so that once another team guesses the identity of the famous person, other teams can still continue to guess the person). Make it clear that each table can only have one guess per clue. Get the scores from each table leader and announce the winner.

Tip: Update the famous people on the slide show to keep it current and relevant for the location and age of the group.

At the end of the activity, say to participants: "Once you get all the facts about a person, you can tell who they are. This week we're going to get some facts from Mark's history of Jesus so we can find out who Jesus really is."

FIVE FACTS
Aim: To show that a person's qualities reveal their true identity.

Equipment: Paper and pen for each group member.

- Give each group member a sheet of paper and a pen.

- Ask them to write the following five things about themselves:
    - Where they were brought up
    - What their best subject is at school/college
    - The furthest place they have travelled
    - Their favourite band
    - What kind of toothpaste they use

- Collect all of the sheets of paper. Read them out, one at a time, asking the group to guess who has written each one.

At the end of the activity, say to participants: "When we gather information about a person, it helps us to identify who they are. This week we're going to get some facts from Mark's history of Jesus so we can find out who Jesus really is."

EXPLORE
◼ *Hand a CY Nano Handbook to each participant. Ask them to turn to page 8 and to write down their answer to this question:*

Think of your best friend. What do you really like about them?

- *Ask a few participants to share their answers. Then point out:* Isn't it interesting that most of you wrote down things about your friend's character and how they behave, rather than commenting on the way they look? It's those things that make our friends important to us.

- Do you know that we don't actually have a physical description of Jesus? But we do know a lot about his character and what he did, and we're going to look at that today. Because those qualities tell us some important things about him.

▶ Ask everyone to turn to **Mark 2:1–12**.

▶ Ask someone to read the passage aloud and then work through the questions below with the group.

Why is the house full at the start of this story? (Look at Mark 1:45 for clues.)

> ◗ People wanted to come and meet Jesus.

> ◗ He was already popular because he had healed the sick and because his teaching was worth hearing.

Imagine you're in the room. How would you have felt when Jesus said: "Son, your sins are forgiven"? (See verse 5.)
Why do you think he said it?

> ◗ It looks as if the man's greatest need is to be healed physically.

> ◗ However, Jesus knows that the man's even greater need is that he should have his sins forgiven and so he deals with this need first.

> ◗ We probably would have only seen the man's physical need. But Jesus saw a deeper need. Jesus knew that the man's sins were more damaging than his disability.

Note: Sin is covered in more detail in Session 3 (CY Jesus came). But in the meantime it might be helpful to think of sin like this: "Shove off God. I'm in charge, Not you!". Point out that sin isn't just the wrong stuff we do, it's also our attitude to God. Sin is a problem because it cuts us off from God and stops us from knowing him.

Why do the religious leaders get so upset when Jesus forgives the man's sin? (See verse 7.) Do you think they are right?

> ◗ They know that sins can only be forgiven by God and so when Jesus says he can forgive sins, he must be claiming to be God.

> ◗ Because sin is against God, only God can forgive it.

> ◗ The religious leaders are partly right, in that only God can forgive sin. But they are also wrong because Jesus is not blaspheming (lying about God): he really is God.

Jesus heals the man so that he can walk. What is the real reason Jesus healed him? (Look at verse 10 for a clue.)

> ◗ Jesus does this to prove that he really does have authority to forgive sins.

> ◗ What Jesus has fixed is the man's relationship with God, so no one can see that the man's sins have really been forgiven. So Jesus does something miraculous that people can see to show that he really does have the power to forgive him.

> ◗ Anyone can claim to forgive another person's sins, but they won't be able to prove they have. Jesus was able to prove he had the authority and ability to forgive sins.

TALK 2

▶ *Deliver Talk 2 using the notes below. The notes for this talk can also be downloaded from www.christianityexplored.org/cy to enable you to adapt them for your group and add your own illustrations. Alternatively, you could show Episode 2 from the Soul DVD if this would be appropriate for your group.*

▶ *There is a recap (called DOWNLOAD) in the participant's CY Nano Handbook for their reference. Encourage people to writes notes on the Download page as they listen to the talk.*

OUTLINE OF TALK TWO: CY JESUS MATTERS

▶ *Use the outline below to develop your own talk. This outline can also be downloaded from www.christianityexplored.org/cy.*

Aim

- ❍ To show that Jesus is God by exploring some events in his life.

- ❍ To show that Jesus can forgive sins, has power to heal, has power over nature, has power over demons and has power over death.

Note: *Keep the pace up as you give this talk – it's a whistle-stop tour, not a full unpacking of every passage!*

Introductory illustration

Choose a person from history who would interest your group, eg: Elvis Presley, Michael Jackson, Martin Luther King, Leonardo da Vinci, Henry VIII, Shakespeare. Ask your group how they would go about finding out about this person. Explain that you are going to find out about Jesus by looking at some of the things he did and said.

Opening

- ❍ Last time, we saw that Christianity is all about Jesus. Mark tells us that Jesus is the "Christ", which means the chosen one of God, God's promised King. Mark also says that Jesus is "the Son of God".

- ❍ Those are pretty amazing claims, so Mark gives us loads of evidence to back them up. He tells us about some of the fantastic things Jesus did and said. We're going to find out about a few of them now, and see what each one shows us about who Jesus is.

▶ **Visual aid:** *Use a visual aid to help the members of your group see how Mark builds up evidence for who Jesus is. This could be written on a white board or large sheet of paper, or displayed using powerpoint. Write or display the heading: "Who is Jesus?" An alternative way to display this information would be to write the headings ("Who is Jesus?" etc) onto slips of paper and then stick them onto the poster from last week's session.*

1. Who is Jesus? Someone who can forgive sins

- ❍ We've already looked at this passage in our groups, but let's read it again together:

▶ *Read aloud **Mark 2:1-12**.*

▶ **Note:** *You know your group. If you think they'll remember this passage well from earlier, then you may prefer to shorten the talk by not reading it again.*

- When Jesus tells the paralysed man that his sins are forgiven, he is really saying two astonishing things:

   1. That he has the authority and ability to forgive sins.

   2. That he is God.

- The religious leaders understood that this is what Jesus was saying – that's why they were so furious with him.

▶ *Act out the following illustration:*
Imagine that I go up to _____ (a leader in the room) and punch him/her in the stomach. But then I turn to _____ (a different leader or a group member) and ask him/her to forgive me. That doesn't work, does it? The only way I can be forgiven for hitting _____ (the first leader) is if he/she forgives me.

- The same is true for our sins. God is the one we sin against. He is the one we hurt. So only God can forgive us.

- The teachers of the law were right when they asked: "Who can forgive sins but God alone?" This means when Jesus says **he** can forgive sins, he's saying that he is God.

▶ **Visual aid:** *Underneath the heading "Who is Jesus?" add "Someone who can forgive sins".*

2. Who is Jesus? Someone who has power to heal

- Imagine again that you're in the room with Jesus. You've seen the roof being torn apart; you've watched a man lowered through the hole and onto the floor; and you've heard Jesus tell the man that his sins are forgiven. Would you believe what Jesus said?

- It would be hard to believe, because nothing seemed to have changed. The man was still lying at Jesus' feet, unable to walk. The religious leaders certainly didn't believe it. They were sure Jesus was just pretending to be able to do what God can do – that's why they were so angry.

- Jesus knew all of that – and so he did something else as well, to show everyone he really does have the same power and authority as God.

▶ *Read aloud* **Mark 2:11-12**.

- This man had needed four friends to carry him to Jesus. But now he was completely well and strong. He was able to stand up, roll his mat up, tuck it under his arm and walk out of the house without anyone helping him.

- No wonder everyone was amazed! They saw that Jesus had the same power to heal that God has. And as Jesus himself pointed out, this proved he had the power to forgive sins, too.

▶ **Visual aid:** *Add "Someone who has power to heal" to your visual aid.*

3. Who is Jesus? Someone who has power over nature

▶ *Tell the story of King Canute, a Viking king of England a thousand years ago, to illustrate the next miracle.*

People often think of King Canute as a foolish king, who thought he could stop the sea from coming in – but actually he wasn't foolish at all; it was his courtiers who were stupid. They were so sure he was the most powerful king around, they even boasted that if he sat in his throne on a beach, the tide wouldn't dare come in and soak him. King Canute knew how foolish this was, so he decided to prove it to them. He arranged for his throne to be set up in the middle of the beach; then he sat down and commanded the sea not to come in. Of course, just as the king knew it would, the sea ignored him and rushed up the shore as usual. The king got wet feet, but he'd made his point to his foolish courtiers.

- ❂ We're going to skip forward to Mark 4 to read about another of Jesus' miracles, and see how different it is from the story of King Canute.

▶ *Read aloud* **Mark 4:35-41**.

- ❂ Unlike King Canute, Jesus really did have power over the sea. In fact, Jesus controlled more than just the sea – he had power over the wind too. He told the wind to stop, and the waves to be still. They both obeyed him!

- ❂ No wonder Jesus' friends were scared! They knew that only God has power over nature. But here was Jesus proving he has exactly the same power as God.

▶ **Visual aid:** *Add "Someone who has power over nature" to your visual aid.*

4. Who is Jesus? Someone who has power over demons

- ❂ Once the storm was over, Jesus and his disciples finished crossing the lake. They landed near a place where a seriously unhappy man lived. His life had been destroyed by evil spirits. These demons made the man so terrifying that the local people tried to keep him tied up. But even when they bound him with chains, he broke loose.

- ❂ When this man saw Jesus, he ran up to him and fell on his knees. The disciples were probably very scared – but Jesus wasn't. He's far more powerful than any demon could ever be.

▶ *Read* **Mark 5:6-17**.

- ❂ When Jesus told the evil spirits they must leave the man, they knew they had no choice. They had to obey Jesus. At his command, they left the man and entered a herd of pigs instead, which rushed down the hill and drowned in the lake.

- ❂ The man himself was still at Jesus' feet. But the demons who'd been destroying his life had left him, and he had now fully recovered. Jesus had saved him.

- ❂ Later, the man went around the area, telling people what Jesus had done for him. They were all amazed when they heard his story, and realised that Jesus had power over the same demons who had scared them so much.

▶ **Visual aid:** *Add "Someone who has power over demons" to your visual aid.*

5. Who is Jesus? Someone who has power over death

- We're going to dip in to one more event from Mark's book. We've already seen that Jesus can forgive sins and has the power to heal. We've also seen he has power over both nature and evil spirits. But now his disciples were going to see Jesus proving his power over something more frightening than any of these – death itself.

- Jesus and his disciples crossed back over the lake, and again were met by a man with a problem. His name was Jairus and he was one of the rulers of the local Jewish synagogue. His problem was that his much-loved daughter was dying.

- Jesus agreed to come at once, but was delayed on the way by someone else who needed his help. No one had been able to help this lady, who had been ill for 12 years. But Jesus could – he healed her completely. But stopping to help the woman had slowed Jesus down. Just as he finished, some men arrived with a horrifying message for Jairus.

▶ Read aloud **Mark 5:35-36**.

- Imagine what that must have been like for Jairus. He's just been told that it's too late, his daughter is dead. But now Jesus is telling him not to be afraid, but instead to believe. That would have been a terrible thing for Jesus to say if he wasn't sure he could back it up. But he was sure. Jairus was about to discover that Jesus has power that only God himself has – power over death.

▶ Read aloud **Mark 5:37-42**.

- When Jesus described this girl as "asleep", he didn't mean that she wasn't really dead – she was. Jairus' servants would have been quite sure about that before coming to him with their sad news. But Jesus knew he could bring the girl back to life just as easily as waking someone who's asleep.

- That's exactly what he did – he spoke to her, and she came back to life immediately. Again, everyone who saw this was astonished – Jesus really had power over death.

▶ **Visual aid:** Add "Someone who has power over death" to your visual aid.

Conclusion

- Mark has shown us five amazing things about "Jesus Christ, the Son of God":
  - Jesus can forgive sins
  - Jesus has power to heal
  - Jesus has power over nature
  - Jesus has power over demons
  - Jesus has power over death

- Everyone who saw Jesus do these things was astonished, because they're things only God himself has the power to do. Only God can forgive sins. Only God has power to heal, to control nature and to command evil spirits. Only God has power over death.

- But Jesus has this power too. Mark is making something very clear to us – that Jesus is God. And if Jesus is God, then can you afford to ignore him?

▶ **Visual aid:** Add "Jesus is God" to your visual aid.

DOWNLOAD

The recap below (called DOWNLOAD) appears in the participant's CY Nano Handbook for their reference.

- Mark 1:1 says that Jesus is the "Christ" – which means the chosen one of God, God's promised King – and "the Son of God". Mark then shows us that:

- Jesus can forgive sins – Mark 2:1-10

- Jesus has power to heal – Mark 2:11-12

- Jesus has power over nature – Mark 4:35-41

- Jesus has power over demons – Mark 5:1-17

- Jesus has power over death – Mark 5:35-42

TALKBACK

▶ *Use the questions below to encourage discussion (they are also printed in the participant's CY Nano Handbook).*

Which of the events Mark tells us about would you have found most amazing or scary? Why?

- This question is designed to get the group talking about the actual events that have been described by Mark and explained by the talk.

- As they are talking about it, try to get them to see the difference between the amazement they would experience seeing a magic trick, say, and the disturbing shock of seeing the things that Jesus did – disturbing because of what they reveal about Jesus.

What do *you* think of Jesus?

- This is a more direct question, although it is okay for people to reserve judgement at this stage by saying: "I'm not sure yet". As the weeks go on, the evidence will become more compelling.

- It may be appropriate at this stage to show why it is simply not right to say that Jesus was "just" a good man, or a teacher, or a religious leader – he must either be a fake, a lunatic or exactly who he claims to be.

▶ *If you have time, now is the moment to answer another of the questions that were asked in the first week's EXPLORE: "If you could ask God one question, and you knew it would be answered, what would it be?" See page 193 for guidance notes on common questions.*

▶ *Be careful that you do not over-run on time. It's always better to leave them wanting more and eager to return next time.*

CONCLUSION

Finish by encouraging your group members to come back next week. Tell them: We've seen some of the amazing things Jesus did and said. Next time we're going to explore what Jesus said about himself.

AFTERWARDS

- ❯ Did any of the group members ask a question or make a comment that you could follow up? If so, plan how you will do that, as well as praying for that person.

- ❯ Is the group talking more than you are? How can you help the quieter ones to open up a little more?

- ❯ Thank God for those who came back this session, and pray that he will open their hearts to the truth about Jesus.

- ❯ Was anyone missing who came last time? Plan to contact them during the week to ask how they are and encourage them to come next time.

3 CY Jesus came

What do you think is the biggest problem facing the world?

From last time's *CY Nano*, what does Jesus think is the biggest problem facing the world?

READ MARK 12:28–31

What does it mean to love God with all your heart, with all your soul, with all your mind and with all your strength?

What does it mean to love your neighbour as yourself?

How good do you think you are at living up to these two commands? Where do you especially mess up?

Do you think sin is a problem? Why or why not?

How would you feel if all your thoughts, words and actions were on display for everyone to see?

What more do I need?

Lovely food...

...great company...

...and beautiful scenery.

15

60

CY Jesus came

> Welcome the group and thank them for coming.

> Recap on the previous session:

Last time we saw some of the amazing things Jesus did and said. We saw that Jesus can forgive sins; that he has power to heal; and that he has power over nature, demons and even death. We saw that Jesus has the same power as God – because Jesus is God.

This time we are going to look at what Jesus said about himself and why he came.

GROUP ACTIVITY

> Choose one of the following activities, to suit your group and the time you have available.

WRONG SKETCH

Aim: To show that everything has a particular purpose.

Equipment: Various household items (eg: a broom, a toothbrush, a wooden spoon, a bucket etc.)

> Give each group two or three items and ask them to prepare a 30-second sketch that makes use of all the items. The only rule is that the items cannot be used as they would normally be used.

> Ask them to perform the sketches to the whole group.

> Example: A possible sketch could be a person coming into a hairdresser's, having their hair brushed with a broom and using the spoon as a mirror.

At the end of the activity, say to your group: "Everything has a proper purpose, doesn't it? If we get that wrong, things can look ridiculous. This week we're going to find out Jesus' true purpose because if we get it wrong, we will be in a worse situation than just looking ridiculous. We're going to see why Jesus came – his mission."

Leader's checklist

Have you...

☐ Reminded the group about the next meeting?

☐ Collected any items needed for the activities?

☐ Enough Bibles or Mark's Gospels for the group?

☐ CY Nano Handbooks and pens for each group member?

☐ Prepared the talk and added any personal illustrations? (Or set up the optional Soul DVD if using it.)

☐ Thought through your answers to the questions?

☐ Invitations to the "Inside Track" weekend/day away?

☐ Prayed for each group member and yourself as the leader?

WRONG EQUIPMENT

Aim: To show that everything has a particular purpose.

Equipment: Large sheets of paper; old magazines; glue sticks

- ❯ Write a job title at the top of each sheet of paper, choosing jobs that need special equipment, eg: dentist, firefighter, hairdresser, cowboy, stuntman.

- ❯ Ask your group to tear out pictures of objects from the magazines and stick them below the job title they may be used for. Encourage them to come up with the funniest suggestions they can.

- ❯ Example: A vacuum cleaner for the dentist or an insect for the cowboy to ride.

At the end of the activity, say to your group: "Everything has a proper purpose, doesn't it? If we get that wrong, things can look ridiculous. This week we're going to find out Jesus' true purpose because if we get it wrong, we will be in a worse situation than just looking ridiculous. We're going to see why Jesus came – his mission."

EXPLORE

▶ *Hand a CY Nano Handbook to each participant. Ask them to turn to page 12 and to write down their answer to this question:*

> **What do you think is the biggest problem facing the world?**

- ❯ Ask the group to share their answers and discuss as appropriate.

- ❯ When possible problems are suggested, see if other members of the group agree and if not, ask them why not.

- ❯ **Note:** *For research on this, or even to do "live" with a projector – type "World's biggest problem" into Google and see what information or illustration you can find.*

> **From last time's CY, what does Jesus think is the biggest problem facing the world?**

- ❯ Get the answer from the group.

- ❯ In Mark 2:1–12 we saw that Jesus did not deal first with the man's disability but with his sin. According to Jesus, the biggest problem facing the world is our sin. (You may want to quickly recap the story of the paralysed man, especially if any of your group missed last week's session.)

- ❯ Recap what was said last week about sin, eg: **S**hove off God. **I**'m in charge, **N**ot you! Sin isn't just the wrong stuff we do; it's also our attitude to God.

▶ *Ask everyone to turn to **Mark 12:28–31**.*

▶ *Ask someone to read the passage aloud and then work through the questions below with the group.*

What does it mean to love God with all your heart, with all your soul, with all your mind and with all your strength?

❯ This means that we put God first in our lives. No one and nothing else can take God's place.

❯ You might need to explain what we mean by "love". Some people might think that you can't choose who you love or even that you cannot control your feelings at all. Here love is more about what you *do* than how you *feel*.

Note: *It may be helpful to give a concrete example of what that means by turning to the first part of the ten commandments (Exodus 20:1–11). For example, you could refer your group to Exodus 20:7 and talk about whether they have ever misused God's name.*

What does it mean to love your neighbour as yourself?

❯ It means that we should treat other people as we would like to be treated ourselves.

Note: *It may be helpful to give a concrete example of what that means by turning to the second part of the ten commandments (Exodus 20:12–17). For example, you could refer your group to Exodus 20:16 and talk about whether they have ever lied to someone.*

❯ Notice that Jesus is not only interested in the way we seem outwardly, but also the way we are deep down, in our hearts and minds. (Older groups may find it helpful to see how Jesus applies Old Testament laws in this way in Matthew 5:21–22 and Matthew 5:27–28.)

How good do you think you are at living up to these two commands? Where do you especially mess up?

❯ This question is designed to help the group see that everyone falls short of these two commands – the two most important of God's commands according to Jesus. This means we're **all** sinners.

❯ You could get the discussion going by admitting that you yourself find it impossible always to obey these two commands. (You probably shouldn't get too specific!) Or you could list how the group members like to be treated by others; then go back over the list asking if that is how they always treat everyone else.

TALK 3

▶ *Deliver Talk 3 using the notes below. The notes for this talk can also be downloaded from www.christianityexplored.org/cy to enable you to adapt them for your group and add your own illustrations. Alternatively, you could show Episode 3 from the Soul DVD if this would be appropriate for your group.*

▶ *There is a recap (called DOWNLOAD) in the group member's CY Nano Handbook for their reference. Encourage people to write notes on the Download page as they listen to the talk.*

OUTLINE OF TALK THREE: CY JESUS CAME

▶ *Use the outline below to develop your own talk. This outline can also be downloaded from www.christianityexplored.org/cy*

Aim

- To explain that Jesus came to deal with our biggest problem: our sin.

- To define sin and show that we all sin.

- To explain the consequences of sin.

- To show that only Jesus can rescue us from our sin.

Opening

- We've seen that Jesus thinks sin is the biggest problem facing the world. We need to find out why he thinks that – but first let's make sure we understand what exactly sin is.

What is sin?

- The most common word for sin in the Bible is a word that means "missing the mark". (If your group would find it interesting, you can tell them that this is the Greek word "hamartavo", which literally means "missing the mark".) Missing the mark can mean both "overstepping the mark" and "falling short of the mark".

▶ *Illustrate this with a simple game. Choose two or three volunteers to come to the front. Give them each three balls (crunched up newspaper is fine); ask them to stand behind a mark (eg: a stick on the floor) and throw their balls into a bucket or bowl three metres away. See how many times they "miss the mark". Alternatively, you could ask them to throw darts (preferably the velcro type) at a dartboard to make the same point.*

- We saw earlier that the two commandments Jesus gave were: "Love the Lord your God with all your heart and with all your soul and with all your mind and with all your strength" and "Love your neighbour as yourself".

- None of us live up to these two commands all the time. We all miss the mark. That's what sin is – missing the mark. Whether we're trying to meet the mark or not, none of us live up to those commands – we all sin.

- But "missing the mark" is far more serious than just missing a target in a game. So another helpful way to understand sin is as rebellion against God (Daniel 9:9).

▶ *You may like to use a crown to illustrate this point (eg: from a child's dressing-up set, or Burger King!). Hold the crown up high and to one side (ie: not above your head). Explain that God is the real King of everyone and everything. He is the loving Creator of our world and is in charge. He is the King. Then put the crown on your head. Explain that we all prefer to be king of our life. We want to be in charge.*

- We want to be in charge; we want to run our lives our own way; we want to make the rules.

- We might choose to eat ten bars of chocolate in a day; or we might choose to share our chocolate with the new boy in our class. But whatever we choose to do (whatever kind of rules we make), we're still running our lives our own way. And people who ignore the king's rules and make their own instead are actually rebels. They're rebelling against their king.

- That rebellion is what the Bible calls "sin".

- Let's find out what Jesus has to say about sin:

▶ Read aloud **Mark 7:20-23**. Explain as you read that the word "unclean" means "unacceptable to God".

- Jesus says the problem comes from inside us – it's in our hearts. We have a heart disease. ("Heart" here doesn't mean the organ that pumps blood – it means who we are and what we're like inside.)

- The wrong things we do and say and think are the outward signs, the symptoms, of this disease – but the actual disease, the real problem, is in our hearts.

- It's our hearts that make us "unclean" – unacceptable to God.

Why is sin our biggest problem?
- There are two reasons why sin is such a problem. The first is that it messes up our relationship with God.

▶ Read aloud **Mark 9:43-47**.

- Jesus warns us here that our sin will lead us to hell. And he says that's so serious it would be better to cut off any part of us that causes us to sin, than to end up in hell!

- God is our loving Creator. He is perfect and totally good. God's our loving King, but we rebel against him. We reject him as our King. Instead, we choose to run our lives our own way, as rebels.

- If we continue to reject God, then he'll respond to our decision – and he'll reject us too. We'll end up separated from him – not just now, but for ever.

- The Bible's name for this eternal separation from God is hell. That's why sin is such a serious problem – because it leads us to hell.

- So the first problem with sin is that it separates us from God and leads us to hell.

- The second problem is that we can't get rid of sin ourselves.

▶ Ask a volunteer to come to the front – choose a leader if group members would find this embarrassing. Give them "measles" by either sticking small red stickers on their face, or using face paint to make red spots. Explain that your poor volunteer now has a very bad case of measles, but it's not a problem because you can fix it. Then produce a packet of sticking plasters/bandaids and stick one plaster over each "spot". Ask whether this would help if it was a real case of measles – why or why not? (Note: check that your volunteer isn't allergic to rubber or plasters. If possible, choose plasters that are easy to remove!)

- Some people think they can fix their sin problem by making sure they don't do anything mean or greedy, and by doing lots of good stuff instead. But that's like sticking plasters over spots. You might be able to hide the spots, but it doesn't deal with the disease inside. Doing good stuff doesn't deal with our sinful hearts.

- So the second problem with sin is that we can't deal with it ourselves.

Jesus came to rescue rebels

- We've seen that sin is a huge problem we can't fix ourselves and which leads us to hell. That's why sin is the biggest problem facing the world.

- But Mark 1:1 tells us that Jesus is "good news". He is good news because he came to rescue rebels.

▶ Read aloud **Mark 2:13-17**.

- Who would you expect Jesus to hang around with? Maybe you'd expect him to spend his time with the good guys. With important people with lots of power. Or maybe with religious leaders.

- But here we see him enjoying a meal with a bunch of sinners – the bad guys!

- Levi was a tax collector. No one who collects money for the government is ever popular. But in those days the tax collectors worked for their enemies, the Romans. And most of them took more money than they should so they could pocket the rest. They were hated crooks.

- But here was Jesus, having a meal with them!

- The religious leaders didn't like what they saw. "Why does he eat with tax collectors and 'sinners'?" they asked.

- Look again at Jesus' answer in verse 17. "It is not the healthy who need a doctor, but the sick. I have not come to call the righteous, but sinners."

- When do you go to see a doctor? It's when you're ill and know you need help. Jesus is saying he came for people who know they are sinners – people who realise they are living as rebels.

- Jesus makes it quite clear he is here for people who realise they're bad, not people who think they're good.

- Jesus came to rescue rebels who know they need his help. He understands the problem of sin and he knows what to do about it. He came to rescue us – and next time we'll see exactly how he does that.

DOWNLOAD

The recap below (called DOWNLOAD) appears in the participant's CY Nano Handbook for their reference.

- Jesus came to deal with our biggest problem: our sin (Mark 2:17).

- Each and every one of us rebels against our loving Creator. That rebellion is what the Bible calls "sin".

- Sin is a serious problem that will lead us to hell. If we continue to reject God, then he will respond to that decision – and reject us.

- Only Jesus can rescue us from the problem of sin. Jesus came to rescue rebels.

TALKBACK

▶ *Use the questions below to encourage discussion (they are also printed in the participant's CY Nano Handbook).*

Do you think sin is a problem? Why or why not?

- ❯ Think about the problems that you have with friends, or about big problems in the world… the root cause is sin.

- ❯ Some group members may not recognize that sin is a problem for them. The next question should help.

How would you feel if all your thoughts, words and actions were on display for everyone to see?

- ❯ The aim here is to help them understand that sin is a problem for them personally.

- ❯ Our sin is a problem: to others (who are hurt by and have to deal with our selfish behaviour); and, most importantly, to God (who will rightly judge us for how we have lived.)

- ❯ In other words, we all break the two most important commands: we all fail to love God and our neighbour as we should.

▶ *Give out invitations to the "Inside Track" weekend/day away, and explain that this will be happening after week 6 of the CY Nano course. See Section 4 on page 161 for details of the "Inside Track" weekend/day way.*

▶ *If you have time, now is the moment to answer another of the questions that were asked in the first week's EXPLORE: "If you could ask God one question, and you knew it would be answered, what would it be?"*

▶ *Be careful that you do not over-run on time. It's always better to leave them wanting more and eager to return next time.*

CONCLUSION

Finish by encouraging your group members to come back next time. Tell them: We've seen why sin is such a huge problem, and that Jesus came to rescue rebels. If sin is the biggest problem we all face, then surely the answer to that problem would be the best and most important news ever. Come back next time to hear it.

AFTERWARDS

- ❯ Did any of the group members ask a question or make a comment that you could follow up? If so, plan how you will do that, as well as praying for that person.

- ❯ Pray that this week the Holy Spirit would do his work of convicting group members that they are sinners under the judgment of God.

- ❯ Thank God for those who came back this session, and pray that he will open their hearts to the truth about Jesus.

- ❯ Was anyone missing who came last time? Plan to contact them during the week to ask how they are and encourage them to come next time.

4 CY Jesus died

Imagine you know how and when you will die. How would it make you feel? What would it make you do?

READ MARK 8:27–33

What does Peter realize in verse 29?

● CY Jesus died

Why would Jesus' words in verse 31 surprise Peter?

Why does Jesus confront Peter in verse 33?

When Jesus died on the cross, was it unexpected? (Look at Mark 9:31 and Mark 10:33–34 for clues.)

How would you feel if someone else deliberately took the punishment for something serious you had done wrong?

Why do you think Jesus' death on the cross is so important to Christians?

Which of the reactions to Jesus' death is most like your reaction?

Hey, want to watch a DVD?

Sure, what is it?

It's my life story, featuring all the best bits.

Why not? I've got 20 seconds to spare.

19

68

CY Jesus died

▶ *Welcome the group and thank them for coming.*

▶ *Recap on the previous session:*
Last time we saw that Jesus came to deal with our biggest problem: our sin. We all sin; we all miss the mark; we all rebel against our loving Creator. We also saw that sin is a serious problem because it leads us to hell, which means being separated from God for ever. Only Jesus can rescue us from the problem of sin. Jesus came to rescue rebels.

This time we are going to find out what happened when Jesus died and how he rescues rebels.

GROUP ACTIVITY
▶ *Choose one of the following activities, to suit your group and the time you have available.*

CELEBRITY PAIRS
Aim: To show that we link certain symbols with certain people.

Equipment: A prize; 18 pieces of paper – 9 with famous people on them and 9 with their associated symbols on them. (For example, you could match Neil Armstrong with the moon, Bill Gates with a computer, the Wright Brothers with an airplane. You can download some suggestions for this game from www.christianityexplored.org/cy).

- Split the group into two teams. The object of the game is to match the famous people to the relevant symbols.

- Place all 18 "cards" face down.

- The teams take it in turns to choose two cards and, if they are not a matching pair, the cards are turned back over.

- 10 points are awarded for each correctly matched pair. The game ends when all pairs have been matched. The team with the most points wins a prize.

Note: For large groups, each table will need their own set.

At the end of the activity, say to participants: "We link different symbols with different people. The cross is often linked with Christians or Jesus. Today we're going to see what actually happened at the cross."

RACE FOR THE RANSOM

Aim: To set up the idea of a ransom, which will be referred to in the talk/DVD.

Equipment: Depends on which version you play.

If you have space, there are various games you can play to introduce the concept of paying a ransom to free a captive. In each case, divide your group into two or more teams. One member of each team becomes a captive – who can be blindfolded and held at one end of the room. A team can't free their captive until they have raised the necessary ransom.

1. Call out a selection of objects that the team has to find and bring to you (eg: four silver coins, a comb, three left shoes, a rubber band and a picture of the captive – could be drawn by the team or maybe taken using a phone camera). As soon as a team has brought all of the objects, they can go and release their captive.

2. The teams run a relay race, maybe including obstacles, to collect "money" (strips of coloured paper) from a box/basket. They have to collect 10 coloured strips and then bring them to where the captives are being held before being allowed to release their captive.

3. If you have plenty of time and access to a suitable outdoor space, finding and releasing a captive (while collecting items to pay the ransom) is a classic "wide game".

At the end of the activity, say to participants: "In our game, the captive couldn't be released until the correct ransom had been paid. Jesus told his followers that he had come 'to give his life as a ransom for many'. Today we'll find out what he meant by that."

EXPLORE

▶ *Hand a CY Nano Handbook to each participant. Ask them to turn to page 16 and to write down their answer to this question:*

> **Imagine you know how and when you will die. How would it make you feel? What would it make you do?**

● This is a question to get people talking. There are no wrong answers, so try to avoid making value judgements on their suggestions.

● Most people would feel terrible knowing when and how they will die. It might make you desperate to try and avoid it (as in Sleeping Beauty, when her father banned spinning wheels from the land because she was cursed to die by pricking her finger on one). Or else you could go mad, do nothing or perhaps "eat, drink and be merry". Some people might spend the remaining time helping others.

Note: Be aware that this question may be a particularly emotive issue for some of your group – especially if they have had a friend or family member die recently. Be extra vigilant for anyone who is troubled by this question, and make sure that you set an appropriate tone for the discussion. You should also offer comfort and support to anyone who is struggling with this issue.

▶ *Ask everyone to turn to **Mark 8:27-33**.*

▶ *Ask someone to read the passage aloud and then work through the questions below with the group.*

What does Peter realize in verse 29?

● Peter realizes that Jesus is the Christ – which means "the anointed one", God's chosen King.

● This is the first time that Peter sees this. This is pretty amazing, considering that he has been around Jesus all the time he was doing miracles, teaching and raising the dead.

Why would Jesus' words in verse 31 surprise Peter?

● It would be surprising to hear that God's King was going to die.

● If it would be helpful to your group, you may want to explain the historical setting. Peter was living in a country that was ruled by the hated Romans. The Jews had been waiting for hundreds of years for God to send the promised Messiah/Christ. They knew the Messiah would be a rescuing King, so they hoped that he would rescue them from the power of the Romans.

Why does Jesus confront Peter in verse 33?

● Peter is told off because he does not think about the "things of God" – in other words, he is thinking about Jesus as King in a human way, not in God's way. He has realized who Jesus is, but he has not understood that Jesus' mission is to come and die.

When Jesus died on the cross, was it unexpected? (Look at Mark 9:31 and Mark 10:33–34 for clues.)

● It wasn't unexpected – Jesus had taught his disciples repeatedly about the way he would die.

TALK 4

▶ *Deliver Talk 4 using the notes below. The notes for this talk can also be downloaded from www.christianityexplored.org/cy to enable you to adapt them for your group and add your own illustrations. Alternatively, you could show Episode 4 from the Soul DVD if this would be appropriate for your group.*

▶ *There is a recap (called DOWNLOAD) in the group member's CY Nano Handbook for their reference. Encourage people to write notes on the Download page as they listen to the talk.*

OUTLINE OF TALK 4: CY JESUS DIED

▶ *Use the outline below to develop your own talk. This outline can also be downloaded from www.christianityexplored.org/cy*

Aim

- ◉ To explain that Jesus knew when he was going to die. His death was no accident – it was planned.

- ◉ To explain that Jesus' death is the only way we can be rescued from God's judgment on our sin.

- ◉ To show that Jesus' death makes it possible for us to be accepted by God and enjoy a friendship with him.

- ◉ To explore the different reactions people have to Jesus' death.

Opening

▶ *Do a quick survey of the group to see how many of them are wearing or carrying some kind of symbol (eg: logos on clothing, bags, mobile phones etc.).*

▶ *Display a cross (eg: on a flipchart or powerpoint slide, or made from card and stuck to the wall).*

- ◉ The cross is the symbol most strongly linked with Christianity. You'll see one inside and outside most churches, and many Christians wear a cross round their necks or pinned to a coat.

- ◉ But it's actually a bit weird to wear a cross as jewellery. It's like wearing an electric chair or a hangman's noose! A cross was an ancient torture device, designed to make death as slow and painful as possible. It's not a cosy symbol or a pretty necklace – it's a way of killing people.

- ◉ Something amazing must have happened to make people choose this terrifying killing machine as their favourite symbol. Well, something amazing did happen – and that's what we're going to be finding out about today.

Why did Jesus die?

- ◉ We've seen in our groups that Jesus knew he was going to die. He even knew when he was going to die. It wasn't an accident. He wasn't tricked. He wasn't surprised.

- ◉ Jesus spent the week before his death in Jerusalem teaching about God. He knew the religious leaders were coming for him. He knew they'd arrange to have him arrested. He knew they'd hand him over to the Romans to be killed. And he was right.

- ◉ Jesus knew when he was going to die. He also knew *why* he was going to die.

▶ *Read aloud **Mark 10:45**, explaining that "the Son of Man" is a title Jesus often used when talking about himself.*

- ◉ Jesus is God's Son, with all the same power as God the Father. But he says here that he came to be a servant. He also says that he came to give his life – to die – as a ransom.

▶ *Illustrate this by asking for a volunteer and then using some thick rope to tie them to a chair. Explain that they can't free themselves – the rope is too thick to break, and they can't reach the knot – and that you'll only release them if a ransom is paid. Set an enormous price, and ask if anyone there is able to pay it. If there's been a recent kidnapping in the news, you might choose to refer to this, to make the point that real ransoms are huge, and the consequences are often deadly if the ransom isn't paid. (Don't forget to untie your volunteer at the end of this illustration!)* **Note:** *Be careful not to cast God as a mean kidnapper demanding a ransom. Referring back to previous weeks should help avoid that.*

❯ Last week we saw why Jesus came – he came to rescue rebels. We also saw that we're all rebels, because we all want to live our lives our way instead of God's way. We rebel against God, our loving King.

❯ Jesus came to rescue rebels – and he rescues rebels by giving his life as a ransom.

What happened when Jesus died?

❯ Mark tells us what happened as Jesus died.

▶ *Read aloud* **Mark 15:22-32**.

❯ Jesus was nailed to a cross of wood and left to hang there until he died. The Romans crucified people in this way as a punishment. Usually only criminals were executed by crucifixion – and, in fact, there were two robbers killed at the same time. There were three crosses in a row, with Jesus in the middle.

❯ Imagine if you'd been there. You'd see three men. All of them bruised and bleeding. All of them stripped of their clothes. All nailed to wooden crosses. They would all look much the same.

❯ But they weren't the same! The two robbers were being punished for the wrong they'd done. But Jesus hadn't stolen anything. He hadn't lied, or cheated, or hurt anyone. Jesus wasn't dying because he'd done wrong things – he was dying as a ransom for many. He was dying to rescue rebels.

❯ But how does Jesus' death rescue rebels? To understand that, we need to see what happened next.

▶ *Read aloud* **Mark 15:33-39**.

❯ After Jesus had been hanging on the cross for three hours, something astonishing happened. It was the middle of the day – but suddenly it was pitch dark, a darkness that lasted for another three hours.

❯ In the Bible, darkness is a picture of God's judgment and anger. This darkness was a sign that God's anger was being poured out on Jesus. But Jesus hadn't done anything wrong – so why was God angry? To understand that, we have to understand what was happening to Jesus while he was on the cross.

▶ *Use the following illustration to show how our sin was put onto Jesus:*

What to do	**What to say**

Hold up a blank DVD case.

Imagine that someone has filmed your life and put it on DVD – but they've just chosen the bad stuff. Every time you've told a lie. Each time you let a friend down or were rude to your mum or dad. All the times you laughed at someone behind their back or took something that wasn't yours. Imagine that they filmed every single wrong thing you did or said or thought. That would be quite a film, wouldn't it? I certainly wouldn't want anyone to see mine – it would show what a rebel I am.

Hold one hand out, with your palm facing the ceiling.

Imagine that this hand is me, and that the ceiling is where God is.

Take the DVD and put it flat on your hand.

This DVD shows all the wrong stuff I've ever done – it shows my sin. But when I put it here (*on your hand*), it gets in the way between me and God. It stops me from knowing God and living as his friend. That's why sin is such a problem – it separates us from God.

Now hold the other hand out.

Imagine that this hand is Jesus. He was perfect. He never did anything wrong – he never sinned. That means that there was nothing at all between Jesus and his Father, God. They had a perfect, loving relationship.

But when Jesus was dying on the cross, this is what happened:

Move the DVD from one hand onto the other.

All my sin was put onto Jesus. He took all my sin, and it separated him from God. That's why he cried out in verse 34: "My God, my God, why have you forsaken me?" For the first time ever, Jesus was separated from his Father. And God then poured out his anger at sin onto his son, as he punished Jesus for our sin.

What to do	**What to say**

But look back at my other hand for a moment. The sin is gone – it's been taken away by Jesus. Now there is nothing separating me from God. This is how Jesus rescues rebels. This is how Jesus gave his life as a ransom for many.

- Jesus willingly went through this brutal death and the terrible separation from his Father. He chose to take the punishment for *our* sin. He was punished in *our* place, so that *we* can be rescued.

- After the three hours of darkness, Jesus gave a loud cry and died. His job was done – he had taken the punishment for our sin, he had paid the ransom for many.

- Now we can see why the cross is so important to Christians. Jesus' death was horrific. But the result of his death is wonderful. Jesus paid the ransom for many, which makes it possible for us to be accepted by God and enjoy a friendship with him.

▸ *You may want to include this question to reinforce this point: Jesus died on a Friday. What do we call that day? (Good Friday.) Jesus' death was brutal. But we call the day he died "good"! Why? Because something incredibly good came out of it. We can be accepted by God, and live as his friends, only because Jesus died as a ransom for many. You could refer back to Session 1, where it was emphasised that Christianity is good news about Jesus. The cross is the greatest example of why Christianity is good news.*

How did people react when Jesus died?
- Mark tells us about a number of people who were around when Jesus died. They all reacted in different ways.

▸ *Use a simple visual aid to show these four people/groups and their four reactions (eg: on a flipchart, labels stuck on the wall or using a powerpoint presentation). Start with the visual aid blank and add each new section as you talk about it.*

Pontius Pilate	Goes with the crowd
The soldiers	Wrapped up in themselves
The religious leaders	Think they don't need Jesus
The Roman centurion	Gets it right

Note: *These four reactions can be applied directly to your group members to help them think about their own response to Jesus. Depending on your group, and also the time you have available, you may choose to do that during this part of the talk, or as part of the final "Talkback" question, or not at all. Some suggestions for application are given in the closing "Talkback" question on page 77.*

1. Pontius Pilate
▸ *Read aloud* **Mark 15:15**.

- Pontius Pilate was the Roman Governor in charge of that part of Israel. He knew Jesus hadn't done anything wrong, but the crowd were yelling and shouting for Jesus to be killed. So Pilate chose to *go with the crowd* – and he handed Jesus over to be crucified.

2. The soldiers

- The Roman soldiers who crucified Jesus were used to executing people this way. They had stripped Jesus and the two robbers of their clothes before crucifying them; so now they played a game to see who would get to keep the clothes. They didn't take much notice of the dying men – they were too *wrapped up in themselves*.

3. The religious leaders

- The religious leaders had hated Jesus for years. They were the ones who had him arrested, and stirred the crowd up to call for his death. They thought God was pleased with them the way they were. They didn't believe they needed rescuing, so they *thought they didn't need Jesus*.

4. The Roman centurion

- The last reaction we'll see came from the Roman centurion who was in charge of the executions. Like the soldiers who worked for him, he had seen loads of people get crucified. But he'd never seen anyone like Jesus. Look again at what Mark tells us.

▶ *Read aloud* **Mark 15:39**.

- The centurion *gets it right*. Jesus, who'd just died in front of him, really is the Son of God. And he came to rescue rebels.

- Four reactions to the death of Jesus: Pontius Pilate goes with the crowd; the soldiers are wrapped up in themselves; the religious leaders think they don't need Jesus; and the Roman centurion gets it right.

- How about you? How do you react?

DOWNLOAD

The recap below (called DOWNLOAD) appears in the participant's CY Nano Handbook for their reference.

- Jesus knew when he was going to die. His death wasn't an accident – it was planned.

- Jesus' death is the only way we can be saved from our sin. It is the way Jesus rescues us, as "a ransom for many" (Mark 10:45).

- When Jesus died, he was willingly taking the punishment for *our* sin. He was punished in *our* place, so that *we* can be rescued.

- Jesus' death makes it possible for us to be accepted by God and enjoy a friendship with him.

- People have different reactions to Jesus' death: Pontius Pilate goes with the crowd; the soldiers are wrapped up in themselves; the religious leaders think they don't need Jesus; the Roman centurion gets it right, when he says that Jesus is "the Son of God".

TALKBACK

▶ *Use the questions below to encourage discussion (they are also printed in the participant's CY Nano Handbook).*

How would you feel if someone else deliberately took the punishment for something serious you had done wrong?

- This could bring out a number of differing reactions:

    - Glad. The other person is a sucker for taking the blame.

    - Guilty. I should have been punished instead.

    - Bad. For the person who suffered.

    - Grateful. Thankful for the person who took your punishment.

- Or any mixture of the above.

- You could follow up with: "What if it is a really bad punishment – not just being told off by a teacher, but actually going to prison?" The question is designed to open up a discussion about guilt, responsibility etc, so there is no need to make any comment about the replies.

Why do you think Jesus' death on the cross is so important to Christians?

- Because the cross is where our sin (our biggest problem) was dealt with.

- At the cross Jesus took the punishment we deserve. It should have been me dying there, but he died in my place.

- If it weren't for the cross, no one could be forgiven! No one could be acceptable to God!

- It also demonstrates God's love (Romans 5:8). If we find it hard to believe God loves us, here is the proof.

Which of the reactions to Jesus' death is most like your reaction?

- Some people might not want to answer this in front of others. You could perhaps ask them to underline the one in DOWNLOAD that is most like their reaction – or start by asking them which reaction they think most of their friends would choose.

- There is an opportunity here to apply these four reactions to the members of your group:

1. Pilate *goes with the crowd*. Young people are often hugely influenced by those around them. They easily give in to peer pressure. Choosing to follow Jesus would mean going his way instead of following the crowd. Are they ready to do that?

2. The soldiers are *wrapped up in themselves*. Young people are often literally wrapped up in their own world, with headphones in their ears and their eyes glued to their mobile phone. It's very easy in this situation to ignore the world around them. But can they afford to ignore Jesus?

3. The religious leaders *think they don't need Jesus*. The religious leaders thought they were good enough for God – that he would accept them as they were. You may want to remind your group that last time we saw that we all sin, that none of us can deal with our sin by ourselves, and that sin leads to hell. Some people feel they are safe because they have Christian parents or have been baptized or confirmed. But religion cannot save us. Only Jesus can.

4. The Roman centurion *gets it right*. We don't know much about this centurion. We know that his reaction at the cross was right – but we don't know how he chose to respond to Jesus afterwards. "Getting it right" isn't just understanding who Jesus is – we also need to put our trust in him to rescue us from the problem of sin and to help us live as his followers.

▶ *If you have time, now is the moment to answer another of the questions that were asked in the first week's EXPLORE: "If you could ask God one question, and you knew it would be answered, what would it be?"*

▶ *Be careful that you do not over-run on time. It's always better to leave them wanting more and eager to return next time.*

CONCLUSION

▶ *Remind the group about the Inside Track weekend/day away. Give out invitations to anyone who was missing last time, or who has lost their invite.*

Finish by encouraging your group members to come back next time. Tell them: We've seen why the death of Jesus is so important to Christians. But what happened next? The Bible tells us that Jesus came back to life again – but would it matter if he hadn't? Next week we'll see why it matters that Jesus came back from the dead.

AFTERWARDS

- Did any of the group members ask a question or make a comment that you could follow up? If so, plan how you will do that, as well as praying for that person.

- Thank God for those who came this session, and pray that he will open their hearts to the truth about Jesus.

- Pray that the Holy Spirit will open blind eyes to see why Jesus died, and why his death matters to them.

- Was anyone missing who came last time? Plan to contact them during the week to ask how they are and encourage them to come next time.

CY Jesus lives

▶ *Welcome the group and thank them for coming.*

▶ *Recap on the previous session:*
Last time we saw why Jesus died. He gave his life as a ransom for many. He was punished in our place so that we can be rescued. His death makes it possible for us to be accepted by God and enjoy a relationship with him. We also saw some of the different ways people reacted to Jesus' death.

This time we are going to think about the resurrection of Jesus – did he really rise from the dead and why does it matter?

GROUP ACTIVITY
▶ *Choose one of the following activities, to suit your group and the time you have available.*

STACK ATTACK
Aim: This activity is intended to help participants see how important Jesus' resurrection is: without it, Christianity would fall apart.

Equipment: One tower of wooden blocks (there are numerous versions of this game available from toy stores).

● Participants take turns to remove a block from the tower, then place it on top of the tower.

● As the game continues, the tower becomes less and less stable until eventually it topples over.

● The person who removes the block that topples the tower loses.

Note: Make sure there is a time limit on this activity by allowing a maximum of 10 seconds to remove each block.

At the end of the activity, say to participants: "All it takes is for one crucial block to be removed, and the tower falls. The reason we're talking about the resurrection of Jesus this week is because it is 'the crucial block' in Christianity."

Leader's checklist

Have you...

☐ Reminded the group about the next meeting?

☐ Collected any items needed for the activities?

☐ Enough Bibles or Mark's Gospels for the group?

☐ CY Nano Handbooks and pens for each group member?

☐ Prepared the talk and added any personal illustrations? (Or set up the optional Soul DVD if using it.)

☐ Thought through your answers to the questions?

☐ Spare invitations to the "Inside Track" weekend/ day away?

☐ Prayed for each group member and yourself as the leader?

EYEWITNESS

Aim: To introduce the idea of eyewitnesses.

Equipment: Paper and pens.

- Choose two volunteers to wait outside the room.

- While they are outside, explain to the rest of the group that the two will come back for just one minute, during which time the group have to look at them very carefully to memorise how they look.

- Call the two volunteers back – but send them out again after one minute.

- Now ask the volunteers to each make three changes to how they look (eg: move a watch or ring to the other hand, untie a shoelace, do up a button…) Ask them to make at least one of the changes very obvious.

- Call the volunteers back and give the group one minute to spot the three changes on each of them and write them down.

- Ask who spotted all six changes, to see who the best eyewitnesses are in your group.

At the end of the activity, say to participants: "Some of us are better eyewitnesses than others when looking for tiny changes – but it was easy to spot the big, obvious changes. Today we're going to be thinking about the death and resurrection of Jesus. A dead man coming back to life is something people would be sure to notice! We will see that there were many eyewitness who saw that Jesus really did die and rise again."

EXPLORE

▶ *Hand a CY Nano handbook to each participant. Ask them to turn to page 20 and to write down their answer to this question:*

> **What would be your first reaction if you heard someone had come back from the dead?**

- Ask the group to share their answers.

- Most will respond that it is impossible, or certainly not believable: dead people do not come back to life again.

- A follow-up question could be to ask: "What would you need to know in order to be convinced that someone had actually risen from the dead?" If people say, "I'd need to see it myself", you might respond, "What if someone you trust had seen it, like a close friend or an eyewitness in a court case?"

Note: *It's actually reasonable to be sceptical about someone coming back from the dead – because no one else has. The fact that Jesus came back from the dead highlights his unique identity – after all, no one else is the Son of God! If your group mention Jairus' daughter, who they read about in Session 2, explain that she was brought back to life for a while, but eventually died again. (The same is true for Lazarus.) Only Jesus has beaten death – the first full and true resurrection.*

▶ *Ask everyone to turn to **Mark 15:42 – 16:8**. (See note on page 87 about verses 9-20.)*

▶ *Tell the group to listen carefully for four things that surprise the women when they arrive at Jesus' tomb.*

▶ *Ask someone to read the passage aloud and then work through the questions below with the group.*

Why are the women worried as they approach the tomb? (See Mark 16:3.)

- ❯ They do not know how they will move the stone.

- ❯ It might be helpful to ask what the women were expecting to find. Then point out that none of Jesus' followers were expecting the resurrection. Jesus had told them, but they hadn't understood what he meant (Mark 9:31-32).

Find four things that surprise them when they arrive. (See verses 4-6.)

1. The stone is rolled away.

2. Jesus is not there.

3. A man in white greets them inside the tomb.

4. He tells them that Jesus is risen.

Should they have been surprised that Jesus rose from the dead? (Look at Mark 8:31, 9:30-31, 10:32-34 for clues.)

- ❯ In all of these passages, Jesus predicts that his resurrection will happen three days after he has been killed.

- ❯ The women should not have been surprised by Jesus' resurrection. In fact, they should have expected it.

Why do you think the women ran away from the tomb?

- ❯ They were amazed that Jesus had risen from the dead, but they were also afraid because they did not expect it.

- ❯ They came looking for "Jesus the Nazarene" – a man from Nazareth – rather than "Jesus Christ, the Son of God".

- ❯ They had seen an angel. We know that angels are frightening because they nearly always begin their message by telling people not to be afraid! Eg: Mark 16:6.

- ❯ You might ask: What would you have thought had happened to Jesus if you came to the empty tomb?

TALK 5

▶ *Deliver Talk 5 using the notes below. The notes for this talk can also be downloaded from www.christianityexplored.org/cy to enable you to adapt them for your group and add your own illustrations. Alternatively, you could show Episode 5 from the Soul DVD if this would be appropriate for your group.*

▶ *There is a recap (called DOWNLOAD) in the group member's CY Nano Handbook for their reference. Encourage people to write notes on the Download page as they listen to the talk.*

OUTLINE OF TALK 5: CY JESUS LIVES

▶ *Use the outline below to develop your own talk. This outline can also be downloaded from www.christianityexplored.org/cy*

Aim

- To explain that Jesus' resurrection is a crucial part of Christianity.

- To investigate the evidence that Jesus really did die and rise again.

- To explore the consequences of Jesus' resurrection.

Opening illustration

▶ *Show the group an object with three legs or wheels, eg: three-legged stool, camera tripod, three-wheeled buggy, child's tricycle. Use an actual object if possible or, alternatively, a picture of one. Ask what would happen if one leg or wheel was removed. (The item would collapse. It might be fun to demonstrate this if you can.) Explain that the same is true for Christianity – if Jesus has not risen from the dead, it would be as if one leg/wheel was missing. The resurrection is crucial for Christians – without it, the whole of Christianity would collapse.*

- Last week, we saw that Jesus came "to give his life as a ransom for many". We saw that his death is the way Jesus rescues rebels.

- Today we're going to find out why the resurrection of Jesus matters so much. But first, we need to be sure Jesus really did die, and that he really did rise from the dead.

Did Jesus really die?

- Jesus died on a Friday afternoon. Soon the sun would go down, which would be the start of the Jewish special day, the Sabbath. This was a day of rest for Jewish people, so there was a rush to get Jesus buried before sunset.

▶ *Read aloud **Mark 15:42-47**. Ask the group to listen carefully to see who was sure that Jesus was really dead.*

- An important man called Joseph of Arimathea went to see the Roman Governor, Pontius Pilate, and asked permission to bury Jesus.

- Pilate was surprised that Jesus was already dead. People who were crucified often took a very long time – even days – to die. He wanted to check it was true, so he called for the Roman centurion who'd been in charge of the execution. The centurion confirmed Jesus was dead, so Pilate allowed Joseph to take the body.

- Joseph had Jesus' body wrapped in a new piece of linen cloth and buried in a stone tomb. The tomb was like a small cave, cut out of the rocky hillside. Jesus' body was put into the tomb, which was then sealed shut by rolling a large stone across the entrance.

⦿ Two of Jesus' friends – two women, both called Mary – watched as Jesus was buried in the tomb.

▶ Ask the group: "By the end of this passage, who was sure that Jesus was dead?" You may want to comment on their answers, in order to reinforce the evidence Mark gives us, eg:

Yes, Joseph was sure – he wouldn't have asked for the body otherwise.
Yes, the Roman centurion was sure – he saw Jesus die with his own eyes.
Yes, Pilate was sure – he checked with the centurion, and he knew the centurion was experienced at executing people.
Yes, the two Marys were sure – they saw Jesus' body buried in the tomb.

⦿ There are three other Gospels in the Bible, which give us even more evidence that Jesus was really dead – but Mark has already given us plenty. We can be sure that Jesus really did die.

Did Jesus really rise from the dead?

▶ Illustrate this next section by showing a biography of a famous person. Choose someone your group will know about (eg: a sportsman or film star), but who is now dead. Public libraries are a good source of popular biographies. Explain that biographies mostly follow the same pattern. They start with someone's birth and childhood. They spend most of their time on the famous or important things that person did as an adult. And then they finish with their death. There's not much left to write after that, because the person's life ended with their death.

⦿ But Jesus' life story is different. There are four biographies of Jesus in the Bible – we've been reading the one by Mark; the three others were written by Matthew, Luke and John. The biographies of Jesus are different because they don't end with his death. They all tell us that Jesus came back to life again.

▶ Read aloud **Mark 16:1-8**.

⦿ We already know that Jesus' body had been wrapped in linen cloth and buried in a stone tomb. Usually, spices would have been put on the body as it was wrapped. That hadn't happened this time – maybe there wasn't time in the rush to finish before the Sabbath began.

⦿ The Sabbath lasted from sunset on Friday evening until sunset on Saturday. Jewish law said the Sabbath had to be a day of rest – so the first chance the women had to go back to the tomb and put spices on the body was early on Sunday morning (Luke 23:55-56).

⦿ We know the women were expecting the body still to be in the tomb – they wouldn't have bothered taking spices with them otherwise. And they wouldn't be worrying about how to move the huge stone if they didn't want to get to the body.

⦿ But when they reached the tomb, the stone had already been rolled away and the tomb was empty. The body wasn't there!

⦿ They didn't find a dead body. Instead they saw a young man dressed in white, an angel – a messenger from God. This angel told the women that Jesus had risen from the dead. He was alive again!

- Later on, Jesus was seen alive by hundreds of people. They were so sure he was alive they couldn't stop talking about him. Many of them were even killed for insisting that Jesus really was alive.

Note: The Bible references for CY all come from Mark's Gospel. However, you may like to check out some of the other evidence for Jesus' resurrection for yourself in Matthew 28:8-20; Luke 24:13-53; John 20:10-31, 21:1-25; Acts 1:1-11, 10:39-43; 1 Corinthians 15:3-7.

- Another piece of evidence for the resurrection is that Jesus himself said it would happen. In Mark 8 Jesus says that he "must be killed and after three days rise again". He says the same thing in chapter 9 and in chapter 10. He knew he was going to die – and he knew he was going to come back to life.

- So the evidence shows that Jesus really did die and then rise again. The vital leg/wheel of the resurrection is true, so Christianity doesn't collapse.

- But why does it matter so much? Why is the resurrection of Jesus so important?

Why did Jesus rise?

- The Bible gives us lots of evidence that proves the resurrection – but it's more interested in what the resurrection proves.

▶ *Use a simple visual aid (eg: on a flipchart or powerpoint presentation) to show the following:*

The resurrection proves that: death has been beaten

Jesus will return to judge everyone

the ransom has been paid

1. Death has been beaten

▶ *Hold up the biography you showed earlier and remind the group that this life story ends with the death of the person the book is about.*

- Everyone who lives will one day die. It's one thing we can be totally certain about – we don't know when we'll die, but we know that we all will.

- But Jesus beat death! He didn't stay dead. He came back to life again. His resurrection shows death isn't the end. Death has been beaten.

2. Jesus will return to judge everyone

- To understand what happens after death, we need to look at something Jesus said before he died.

- After Jesus had been arrested, and before he was led to Pontius Pilate, he was questioned by the Jewish high priest. Jesus had something very important to say about what would happen in the future.

▶ *Read aloud **Mark 14:61b-63**.*

- The high priest was outraged by what he heard – so steamed up that he tore his clothes to show his fury. But why was he so angry?

- When Jesus spoke about "the Son of Man ... coming on the clouds of heaven", he was talking about "The Day of Judgment". This is a day when everyone who has ever lived will have their lives judged. Jesus was saying that no matter what the high priest did to him, Jesus would be the one coming as Judge on the Day of Judgment. No wonder the high priest was furious!

- The Day of Judgment is a day when our sin will be fully displayed and we will be seen as the rebels we truly are.

- This is actually good news. If you've ever felt it's unfair that murderers and rapists seem to get away with it – the answer is that they won't. Every single person who's ever lived will be judged.

- Once, when the apostle Paul was speaking in Athens, he said that God "has set a day when he will judge the world with justice by the man he has appointed. He has given proof of this to all men by raising him from the dead" (Acts 17:31). The resurrection of Jesus is actually proof that the Day of Judgment will come – and that Jesus himself will be the Judge.

3. The ransom has been paid

- Of course, we will be judged on the Day of Judgment as well. We're rebels too. Every wrong thing we've said or done or thought – every time we have turned our backs on God – will be judged too. Without Jesus we would all be found guilty. But Jesus came to rescue rebels.

- Jesus said he came to give his life as a ransom for many. But how do we know the ransom was accepted? Because God brought Jesus back to life.

- God accepted Jesus' death as payment in full for our sins. Jesus died in our place. He took the punishment we deserve. When God brought Jesus back to life, he showed that he accepted Jesus' death as the ransom for many, the way for us to be forgiven (Romans 4:25).

- You can see why the resurrection is so important to Christians. It shows that those who trust in Jesus have no need to fear death and judgment. If we trust in Jesus, we can have confidence that God will raise us from death. Jesus has beaten death and the ransom has been paid.

DOWNLOAD

The recap below (called DOWNLOAD) appears in the participant's CY Nano Handbook for their reference.

- If Jesus has not risen from the dead, Christianity collapses.

- The resurrection proves that Jesus is who he says he is, and that his death was a ransom for many.

- Jesus did die: Pontius Pilate, the Roman centurion, Joseph of Arimathea and the women were all certain that Jesus had died.

- Jesus did rise: the tomb was empty; Jesus was seen alive by hundreds of people, many of whom were later killed for insisting that he was alive.

- The resurrection proves that Jesus will come again as Judge of the whole world (Acts 17:31).

- The resurrection means that death has been defeated. If we trust in Jesus, we can be sure that God will raise us from death.

TALKBACK

▶ *Use the questions below to encourage discussion (they are also printed in the participant's CY Nano Handbook).*

What part of the evidence for Jesus' resurrection do you find most convincing? Why?

- This is to stimulate a general discussion on the evidence.

- Encourage the group to think through the alternatives, eg: "Couldn't Jesus have just fainted?" Answer: No – he'd been through torture, crucifixion and had been stabbed with a spear. The Romans were experts at this – killing was their business. Even if he had simply fainted, could he have rolled back the large stone, avoided a Roman guard and appeared fit and well to his followers soon after? The Roman guard would have been very careful not to let anyone in or out of the tomb, because they knew they might be killed as punishment for failing to do their job properly.

Do you think that Jesus rose from the dead? Why or why not?

- Let people volunteer their answers.

- But if anyone says "no", it's worth gently probing why they don't believe it. Is it that the evidence is not good enough – or is it because they are worried about the implications for them if it is true?

Why does Jesus' resurrection matter, if at all?

- It matters because, if the resurrection happened as Jesus said it would, then we can trust Jesus on every other point. Jesus is who he says he is. Jesus *did* achieve what he said he would on the cross.

- Questions about life after death are no longer a matter of opinion – Jesus is able to answer the question, because he has been there and come back.

- Jesus' resurrection shows that God has accepted Jesus' death as a ransom for many.

- It also shows that Jesus rules over everyone and everything – even death – and proves that he will return to judge the whole world (Acts 17:31).

Note: *You could unpack this question a bit more by asking:* Why, if you trust in Jesus, is the resurrection reassuring? Why, if you don't trust in Jesus, is the resurrection frightening?

▶ *If you have time, now is the moment to answer another of the questions that were asked in the first week's EXPLORE: "If you could ask God one question, and you knew it would be answered, what would it be?"*

▶ *Be careful that you do not over-run on time. It's always better to leave them wanting more and eager to return next time.*

CONCLUSION
▶ *Remind the group about the Inside Track weekend/day away. Give out invitations.*

Finish by encouraging your group members to come back next time. Tell them: We've seen why the resurrection of Jesus is so important to Christians. Next session we're going to explore how the death and resurrection of Jesus makes a difference to our lives.

AFTERWARDS

- ❯ Did any of the group members ask a question or make a comment that you could follow up? If so, plan how you will do that, as well as praying for that person.

- ❯ Thank God for those who came this session, and pray that he will open their hearts to the truth about Jesus.

- ❯ Pray that the group members will be able to attend the Inside Track weekend/day away.

- ❯ Was anyone missing who came last week? Plan to contact them during the week to ask how they are and encourage them to come next time.

Note on Mark 16:9-20
Your group may ask you about the note in their Bibles which says that some early manuscripts do not include Mark 16:9-20. If so, explain that Mark almost certainly didn't write these verses. He finished his Gospel on the cliffhanger of verse 8. The extra verses were probably added early on by a well-meaning scribe who was making a copy of Mark's Gospel. However, it's worth pointing out that all of the information included in verses 9-20 can also be found elsewhere – either in the other Gospels or Acts – so it's not new or invented material, just a summary of what the rest of the Bible says about the evidence for Jesus' resurrection.

If your group don't ask about these verses, then avoid unnecessary confusion by not mentioning them!

6 CY God accepts us

What things do people do so others will accept them?

What things do people do to be accepted by God?

READ MARK 10:17–22

Why does the man think God should accept him?

What is Jesus' response?

Why does the man leave? What does that show about the man?

CY God accepts us

What exactly is grace? How would you explain it if someone asked you?

What do people find offensive about grace? What does it say about us?

What is so great about grace? What does it offer us?

What does grace tell us about what God is like?

What am I going to do? They'll be here any minute!

Calm down. I know just what to do.

Thanks a lot, sis.

CY God accepts us

27

CY God accepts us

▶ *Welcome the group and thank them for coming.*

▶ *Recap on the previous session:*

Last time we looked at the evidence for the resurrection and saw that Jesus really did die and then rise to life. We also saw why his resurrection matters: that it proves that death has been beaten, that Jesus will come back to judge everyone, and that God has accepted the ransom that Jesus paid.

This time we are going to see how this makes a difference to our lives.

GROUP ACTIVITY

▶ *Choose one of the following activities, to suit your group and the time you have available.*

SPAGHETTI TOWERS

Aim: To illustrate what God's grace means.

Equipment: Long spaghetti; bananas; pears; two chocolate bars.

- ● Divide the participants into groups and give each group a packet of spaghetti, one banana and one pear. Tell them that they must build a tower 2 metres high using only these items. They can choose to have their banana or pear cut up by one of the leaders but once it is cut they are not allowed a whole piece of fruit again. Tell them that if they succeed, they win a chocolate bar.

- ● After a while, go to each group offering help. They will probably refuse at first, but one group will ask for help eventually. (If no one asks for help, become more and more keen to offer.) When the first group asks for help, tell them that the task is actually impossible to achieve, no matter how hard they try. Then tell them: "However, because you've asked for help, I'm going to give you two chocolate bars, as a gift."

- ● The game ends after a group asks for your help. That group is declared the winner and given two chocolate bars.

At the end of the activity, say to your group members: "Some things are impossible for us to do, no matter how hard we try. It wasn't possible to build a spaghetti tower because the fruit makes the spaghetti go all weak and wobbly. The only way to get the prize in this case was to realise we couldn't do it, and admit it."

QUIZ

Aim: To illustrate what God's grace means.

Equipment: Quiz questions based on the previous CY Nano sessions, prizes for winner(s) and loser(s) – all the prizes should be the same.

- ❯ Either ask for two volunteers or divide your group into two teams.

- ❯ Offer something your group members will really like as a prize, eg: an I-Tunes voucher or a free cinema ticket for an individual winner, or chocolate bars for the winning team.

- ❯ Base your quiz questions on what's been covered so far during CY Nano (this makes the illustration a useful opportunity to recap what's been learned about Jesus). If both contestants have the same score at the end, ask a tie-breaker question to find the winner (the first hand up with the correct answer).

- ❯ Congratulate the winner and give them a prize – and then give a prize to the loser as well!

At the end of the activity, say to your group members: "Did that seem unfair to you? They didn't deserve a prize did they? But that's a picture of what we're thinking about today – God's grace. Grace is God's undeserved gift to us."

EXPLORE

▶ *Hand a CY Nano Handbook to each participant. Ask them to turn to page 24 and to write down their answer to this question:*

What things do people do so others will accept them?

- ❯ This question is intended to get the group thinking about acceptance.

- ❯ In general, our sinful world tends to accept people because they have achieved something or because they act or dress in a certain way. It is *conditional* acceptance. We are accepted because of something that we do, or say. When we stop doing that thing, we stop being accepted.

Note: *Don't let this discussion get too long or deep. The aim is simply to start with a few concrete examples from their own experience before moving on to consider the issue of being accepted by God. But do be aware of anyone who may be finding the subject of acceptance difficult – this might be something to follow up with them at another time.*

What things do people do to be accepted by God?

- ❯ This question should reveal something about how people think they should approach and be accepted by God.

- ❯ Typical answers might include: going to church; being baptized; doing the right things; having Christian parents.

▶ *Ask everyone to turn to* **Mark 10:17-22**.

▶ *Ask someone to read the passage aloud and then work through the questions below with the group.*

Why does the man think God should accept him?

- ❯ He claims that he has kept the commandments since he was a boy (verse 20). He thinks that God should accept him because he has kept this set of rules.

What is Jesus' response?

- ❯ Jesus tells him that he should go and sell all he has and give money to the poor. And then follow him.

Why does the man leave? What does that show about the man?

- ❯ The man leaves because he does not want to do what Jesus has asked him. He has a lot of money and chooses this above following Jesus.

- ❯ Jesus has shown the man that he has broken the very first commandment (see Exodus 20:2–3). He had made money into a god – it was more important to him than his Creator.

- ❯ Like the man, people sometimes think God will accept them because of good things they've done. But like the man, however good we think we are, we all put "things" in place of God (eg: popularity, image, comfort, good grades, money etc).

Note: *Jesus is not teaching that Christians should have no money. He is teaching that money should not take the place of God – and if something does, we should remove it from our lives. Jesus isn't teaching that giving money would earn God's favour either – rather, he is showing that money was the thing keeping the man from following Jesus.*

TALK 6

▶ *Deliver Talk 6 using the notes below. The notes for this talk can also be downloaded from www.christianityexplored.org/cy to enable you to adapt them for your group and add your own illustrations. Alternatively, you could show Episode 6 from the Soul DVD if this would be appropriate for your group.*

▶ *There is a recap (called DOWNLOAD) in the participant's CY Nano Handbook for their reference. Encourage people to write notes on the Download page as they listen to the talk.*

OUTLINE OF TALK 6: CY GOD ACCEPTS US

▶ *Use the outline below to develop your own talk. This outline can also be downloaded from www.christianityexplored.org/cy*

Aim

- ❯ To illustrate the fact that most people think God will accept them because of things they have or haven't done.

- ❯ To show that God accepts us by grace alone.

- ❯ To define grace.

Opening

▶ *Ask your group to think carefully about the following question and to write down their answer. Assure them that no one will ask what they've written. There is space to write their answer on page 26 of the CY Nano Handbook. The question is:*

If God asked you: "Why should I give you eternal life?", what would you say?

Give the group a couple of minutes to write down their answers.

- ❯ I'm not going to ask you what you wrote – but this is how most people would start…

    You should give me eternal life because I…

- ❯ The answer would then give different reasons why you deserve eternal life. They might be to do with…

    - ❯ *My family or country:* "because my parents are Christian"; "because I was born here"

    - ❯ *The bad things I've never done:* "I've never killed anyone:"; "I don't steal"; "I've never hurt anyone"

    - ❯ *The good things I have done:* "I'm kind to animals, my friends etc"; "I give to charity"

    - ❯ *"Religious" things I do:* "I go to church or to this group", "I believe in God", "I've been baptised", "I read my Bible and pray"

- ❯ There are loads of possible answers – but they're all about something *you* have done or not done.

- ❯ But we've seen in the last few weeks that sin is a heart disease – it comes from inside us. At heart we're all rebels – and no matter how many "good" things we do, we can't clean up our own hearts.

- ❯ The Bible tells us that everyone sins, and therefore *no one* is acceptable to God. No one deserves eternal life!

▶ *Here you could use the illustration of the good sailor. Talk about a sailor on a ship who is brilliant at what he does. He always helps his shipmates. He always obeys the captain's orders. He's a good sailor. But the ship he sails in has a skull and crossbones flying from the mast. He's a pirate! It's the same with us. Even if we're great people, we're still rebels, and will be judged by God.*

◉ So how is it possible for us to be rescued?

Asking Jesus for help
◉ Mark tells us about a man who understood that Jesus was the only one who could help him.

▶ *Read aloud* **Mark 1:40**. *(You could get some leaders or group members to act this out to add interest, if you think it would work with your group.)*

◉ This man had a disgusting skin disease. His face and body were covered with sores no one could cure. This skin disease made him "unclean". That meant he was an outcast – not allowed to live near anyone who was healthy. He couldn't eat food with them, or even touch them. His disease cut him off completely from friends and family. It cut him off from God, too. Someone who was "unclean" wasn't allowed in the temple or a synagogue.

◉ There was no cure for this skin disease. No doctor could help him. He probably could have tried to cover it up himself – hide his skin underneath clothes or even smeared himself with mud so he looked dirty rather than ill! But the truth was that even if he tried to hide it, the disease was still there. There was nothing he could do to get rid of it.

◉ So the man did the only sensible thing he could do – he asked Jesus for help. He asked Jesus to make him "clean".

▶ *Read aloud* **Mark 1:41-42**.

◉ When the man asked Jesus for help, he was asking the only person who could help him. You can see how much Jesus cared for this man. He was full of compassion as he reached out and touched him. This was probably the first time this man had been touched for years – no one else would risk it. But Jesus knew he wasn't going to catch this man's disease – instead he cured it. "Be clean!" he said, and healed the man instantly.

◉ What did the man do to get well? Did he try and fix the problem himself? Did he buy some pills from a doctor? Did he do anything to *deserve* Jesus' help? No. All he did was ask. He asked for help from the one person who could give it.

◉ We're all like that man. His skin disease made him "unclean". It cut him off from family and friends, and also from God. Only Jesus could make him "clean". Our disease isn't a skin disease – but it still makes us unclean. Our sin cuts us off from God. Like the man with the skin disease, we need to ask Jesus to make us clean.

Cut off from God
◉ In the past few weeks we've used different pictures to help us understand the problem of sin. We've tied someone up as a hostage to think about the ransom that needs to be paid, and we've given someone measles to show that covering up the red spots doesn't cure the actual disease. But we don't need to invent a picture to show how sin cuts us off from God – because God has already made one!

▶ *Display the following diagram (see page 94) to show the pattern for the temple. If you have access to a white- or blackboard, use this so that you can rub out the curtain at the appropriate time. Alternatively, prepare two versions of this diagram (eg: on a powerpoint slide) so that you can show what happens.*

- About 1000 years before Mark wrote his Gospel, God gave instructions to his people, the Israelites, to build a temple. It reminded the Israelites that they were God's people and God was with them. But it also had to show them that God is holy and perfect, and that nothing impure can come near to him. There was a room at one end, divided into two smaller rooms by a thick, heavy curtain. No one was allowed through that curtain into the room beyond, called the Most Holy Place. Only one man, the high priest, was allowed inside – and even he was only allowed in once a year.

- The curtain was there as a picture – to show that sin cuts us off from God. It was like a big "Do not enter" sign – a visual aid to remind people of the problem of sin.

The temple curtain

- Why have we started thinking about curtains and temples? Because Mark tells us something wonderful about what happened when Jesus died.

▶ *Read aloud* **Mark 15:37-38**.

- The curtain in the temple is a picture of us being "unclean", unacceptable to God, cut off from him by our sin. But when Jesus died, God ripped the curtain in two, from top to bottom.

▶ *Either rub out the curtain from your diagram or display the version that shows that the curtain has been torn apart.*

- This torn curtain is a wonderful picture of the way Jesus rescues rebels. Jesus' death paid the ransom for sin. He died on the cross in our place, taking the punishment we deserve. When the temple curtain was ripped in two, it showed God had accepted the ransom price. The way to God has been torn open. Anyone who trusts in Jesus can be forgiven.

- You can see why we don't need to invent a visual aid – God has already given us a brilliant one. And remember that God first gave instructions for this visual aid 1000 years before Jesus was born. All those years ago, God knew he was going to send his Son to die on a cross in our place. It was always his plan – and he designed a room with a curtain to help us understand it.

Understanding grace

- Think back to the rich man we read about earlier. His question to Jesus was: "What must I *do* to inherit eternal life?" But there is nothing we can *do* to earn eternal life. God doesn't accept us because of anything we do. Instead, we need to be like the other man, the one with the skin disease. He knew he couldn't help himself. So he fell on his knees in front of Jesus, and asked Jesus to help him.

❂ The man with the skin disease was cut off from God and from other people. He was "unclean" and totally unable to do anything about it himself. So he asked for help, and Jesus made him clean. The man didn't deserve help – it was an undeserved gift from the only one who could help him, Jesus Christ.

❂ We all have a disease too – the disease of sin – which cuts us off from God. We're unclean and totally unable to do anything about it ourselves. We need to ask Jesus for help, to make us clean. We don't deserve his help – we can't do anything to earn it – it's offered to us as an undeserved gift from the only one who can help us, Jesus Christ.

▸ *Display a visual aid showing the word "Grace" and a picture of a wrapped gift.*

❂ The word the Bible uses for this is *grace*. Grace is God's undeserved gift to us. It is God's amazing kindness to us in spite of our rebellion. It is God treating us in a way we don't deserve because of what Jesus has done.

❂ Everything we have learned about who Jesus is and why he came – about his death and his resurrection – happened because God planned it that way. He sent Jesus to rescue rebels. He sent his own Son to die on the cross in our place. He sent his Son as a loving, undeserved gift to us.

❂ And there's something else wonderful about grace. If God accepts me because of what *Jesus* has done, and not what *I* have done, then it means he still accepts me, even when I mess up.

▸ *Illustrate this with the following example: "Most of you know what it's like if you do something you're really ashamed of. Maybe you've stolen something, or told a nasty lie about someone. You can't bear what your friends would say if they knew, so you keep it to yourself. You have to pretend you've done nothing wrong because you're so scared of what they'll do if they find out."*

❂ We can't hide anything from God – and we don't need to. We can be real with him. If God accepts us because of what Jesus has done, then he will still accept us when we mess up. If we trust in Jesus, God will forgive us and our relationship with him isn't spoiled. That's grace – God's loving, undeserved gift to us.

▸ *Tell the group to look again at what they've written in their books as their answer to:* **If God asked you: "Why should I give you eternal life?", what would you say?**

❂ If what you've written starts with "because I…", then you haven't really understood what Christianity is all about. This is not an answer God accepts.

❂ But if your answer starts "because Jesus…", then perhaps you're beginning to understand that trusting in Jesus is the *only answer that God accepts*. We can only be saved by God's grace – his loving, undeserved gift to us.

▸ *You might like to illustrate the final point of this talk by writing out the types of answers your group might give onto pieces of paper – and then shredding the ones that don't lead to eternal life.*

DOWNLOAD

The recap (called DOWNLOAD) below appears in the participant's CY Nano Handbook for their reference.

- Most people think God will accept them because of things they have done or haven't done. But these things can't solve the problem of sin.

- The Bible tells us that God accepts us, not because of anything *we've* done, but because of what *Jesus* has done.

- Like the man with the skin disease, we need to ask Jesus to make us clean (Mark 1:40-42).

- The only way we can be accepted by God is because he sent Jesus to die on the cross in our place.

- Grace is God's undeserved gift to us. Because of what Jesus has done, God treats us in a way we don't deserve.

TALKBACK

▶ *Use the questions below to encourage discussion (they are also printed in the participant's CY Nano Handbook).*

What exactly is grace? How would you explain it if someone asked you?

- Grace is God's undeserved gift to us.

- We deserve to be punished for our sin, but grace is God forgiving us when we don't deserve it.

What do people find offensive about grace? What does it say about us?

- It tells us that we are hopeless and helpless without it.

- Many people hate this idea – we tend to be proud of ourselves and of our own achievements.

What is so great about grace? What does it offer us?

- The free gift of eternal life.

- It offers us new life, freedom to follow God, a fresh start with Jesus in control, etc.

- It means we can be real with God and not try to hide our mistakes when we mess up.

What does grace tell us about what God is like?

- He is amazing! He is prepared to forgive me, welcome me into his family, and he himself has paid the price of my wrongdoing through the death of Jesus on the cross.

CONCLUSION

▶ *Remind the group about the Inside Track weekend/day away – and confirm any travel arrangements.*

Finish by encouraging your group members to come to the Inside Track weekend/day away, and also to come back next time. Tell them: We've seen that forgiveness is a gift, paid for by Jesus Christ. Next time we're going to find out exactly what it means to be a Christian.

AFTERWARDS

❯ Did any of the group members ask a question or make a comment that you could follow up? If so, plan how you will do that, as well as praying for that person.

❯ Thank God for those who came this time, and pray that he will open their hearts to the truth about Jesus.

❯ Pray that the Holy Spirit will convict group members of their need to accept the gift of forgiveness. If any are already Christians, pray that they will grow in their understanding of God's grace and have the courage to talk openly about their faith in Jesus.

❯ Pray that the group members will be able to attend the Inside Track weekend/day away. Plan to follow up any who haven't let you know whether they are coming.

Inside Track

The *Inside Track* weekend/day away is an important part of the *CY Nano* course as it will give your group members an opportunity to count the cost of being a Christian and consider the implications for their own lives. The *Inside Track* material is designed to be used in between Sessions 6 and 7 of the course.

The weekend/day away will give more time to find out about what it's like being a Christian, and the gifts God gives us to help us live for him. The following four themes will be covered:

- ❯ Introduction: CY it's tough to follow Jesus

- ❯ Session 1: CY we need the Holy Spirit

- ❯ Session 2: CY the church is your family

- ❯ Session 3: CY it's good to talk *(the Bible and prayer)*

Being away together allows more time for reflection and for personal testimonies as your group gets an "inside track" on what it's like being a Christian. It will also give them time to observe how you and your co-leaders live out your own faith in Jesus. They will get part of their "inside track" by looking at you!

You will find all the material for the *Inside Track* weekend/day away in Section 4 of this Leader's manual, starting on page 161.

7 CY we should believe

We started *CY Nano* by asking: "If you could ask God one question, what would it be?"
If God were to ask you one question, what do you think it would be?

READ MARK 1:14–15

What do you think Jesus means by "the good news of God"?

What does Jesus mean when he says: "The time has come" and "The kingdom of God is near"?

What do you think the word "repent" means?

What do you think it means to "believe the good news"?

How would you score the following statements?
(0 = completely unconvinced, 10 = very sure)

Jesus is God

Jesus came to rescue us from our sin.

Following Jesus means denying ourselves
and putting Jesus first, whatever the cost.

What choices will you make
now that you've finished
CY Nano? What are you going
to do next?

What do you see,
the hideous woman or
the beautiful one?

Some people are
just too easy,
aren't they?

7 CY we should believe   37

CY we should believe

▶ *Welcome the group and thank them for coming.*

▶ *Recap on the previous session:*
Last time we saw that God accepts us not because of anything *we've* done, but because of what *Jesus* has done. Like the man with the skin disease, we need to ask Jesus to make us clean. We thought about grace – God's undeserved gift to us – and we saw that forgiveness is a gift, paid for by Jesus.

If you did the Inside Track programme after week 6, also include this summary: And we saw on our weekend/day away that the Christian life is brilliant, but tough.

This time we are going to find out exactly what it means to be a Christian.

GROUP ACTIVITY
▶ *Choose one of the following activities, to suit your group and the time you have available.*

TANGRAMS
Aim: To show that you need to put all the pieces together to make a complete picture.

Equipment: Set of tangram pieces for each team (you can buy these from a toy store or download them from the internet); a prize; powerpoint projector; slide show which you can make yourself or download from www.christianityexplored.org/cy

- ❯ Split the participants into two or three teams and give each team a set of tangram pieces. Display in turn each shape that they must try to make. Remind them that they must use all their pieces.

- ❯ Award the fastest team 10 points and the second fastest team 5 points for each of the shapes they make. If you have three teams, give the slowest team 3 points.

- ❯ Show the solution on the screen.

- ❯ The winning team is the one with the most points and wins the prize.

Leader's checklist

Have you...

- ☐ Collected any items needed for the activities?

- ☐ Enough Bibles or Mark's Gospels for the group?

- ☐ CY Nano Handbooks and pens for each group member?

- ☐ Prepared the talk and added any personal illustrations? (Or set up the optional Soul DVD if using it.)

- ☐ Thought through your answers to the questions?

- ☐ Details of things the group members might choose to do next?

- ☐ Prayed for each group member and yourself as the leader?

At the end of the activity, say to your group: "To get the picture right, we have to put the pieces together in the right way. That's what we'll be doing today as we put together all the pieces we've collected over the past seven sessions."

FOLLOW THE LEADER

Aim: To show that following Jesus will make a difference to how we live and will be noticed by others.

Equipment: None.

- ❯ Sit the group in a circle facing inwards. Ask a volunteer to leave the room.

- ❯ Choose a "leader" from the group. This "leader" starts an action which everyone else copies.

- ❯ Bring the volunteer back in to the room and ask them to stand in the middle of the circle.

- ❯ The "leader" keeps changing their action regularly, with the rest of the group copying the "leader" each time. The volunteer in the middle has to watch carefully and try and work out who the "leader" is.

- ❯ A variation on this game is to ask the "leader" to choose actions with a particular theme, eg: playing different instruments, doing different dance moves, playing different sports.

At the end of the activity, say to your group: "Today we're going to be thinking about following Jesus. If we follow Jesus, it will make a difference to everything we do and other people will notice those differences."

EXPLORE

▶ *Hand a CY Nano Handbook to each participant. Ask them to turn to page 34 and to write down their answer to this question:*

> **We started CY by asking: "If you could ask God one question, what would it be?" If God were to ask *you* one question, what do you think it would it be?**

- ❯ This question will reveal how much your group has absorbed over the last seven weeks. You might get things like:

  - ❯ What is stopping you from believing in me?

  - ❯ Why haven't you put your trust in Jesus?

  - ❯ Why don't you tell others about me?

- ❯ If you get a silly answer, welcome their comment, but try and draw people back to the serious question. It might help to rephrase the question as: "If God were to ask you one question about your faith or relationship with him, what would it be?"

- ❯ As this is the final session you should follow up by asking your group: "How might you answer God if he asked you that?"

▶ *Ask everyone to turn to* **Mark 1:14-15**.

▶ *Ask someone to read the passage aloud and then work through the questions below with the group.*

What do you think Jesus means by "the good news of God"?

❯ This question helps to reveal if your group has understood what the gospel is.

❯ It is the good news that Jesus, God's Son, came into this world, lived a perfect life, died for us on the cross, rose from the dead and is in heaven today. It is the good news that whoever repents and believes in him will be "ransomed from judgment", accepted by God and enjoy a relationship with him forever.

What does Jesus mean when he says: "The time has come" and "The kingdom of God is near"?

❯ It is like saying: "This is it" – the time that everyone has been waiting for is here.

❯ God's kingdom – his power and authority over everything – is being shown in Jesus' life, death and resurrection.

What do you think the word "repent" means?

❯ We haven't discussed repentance yet in the course, but your group members may have some ideas about what it means. If they think it just means "saying sorry", help them to understand its fuller meaning by explaining the following points:

  ❯ Repentance is a complete inner change of our attitude towards God and other people.

  ❯ It begins with a sincere apology to God for our sin because we realize that it has offended him. We then turn from living our own way and start to live God's way.

  ❯ That means being *for* what Jesus is *for*, and *against* what he is *against*.

❯ You could illustrate repentance as completely turning around *from* having your back to God, *to* facing him and walking towards him; living a life that has him as the goal of all that we do. You can act out turning around, which helps communicate the point.

What do you think it means to "believe the good news"?

❯ To believe means more than just saying something is true. It means:

  1. We know about Jesus and what he has done.

  2. We are convinced that these things about Jesus are true.

  3. We place our trust in Jesus and obey him.

  4. Our relationship with him shows who he really is – the Lord. We do as he does, and think as he thinks.

● Believing is more than "knowing" the truth – it means "living" the truth.

TALK 7

▶ *Deliver Talk 7 using the notes below. The notes for this talk can also be downloaded from www.christianityexplored.org/cy to enable you to adapt them for your group and add your own illustrations. Alternatively, you could show Episode 7 from the Soul DVD if this would be appropriate for your group.*

▶ *There is a recap (called DOWNLOAD) in the participant's CY Nano Handbook for their reference. Encourage people to write notes on the Download page as they listen to the talk.*

OUTLINE OF TALK 7: CY WE SHOULD BELIEVE

▶ *Use the outline below to develop your own talk. This outline can also be downloaded from www.christianityexplored.org/cy*

Aim

● To remind people who Jesus is – his identity.

● To remind people that Jesus came to die – his mission.

● To explain that a Christian "must deny himself and take up his cross and follow [Jesus]" (Mark 8:34) – Jesus' call.

Opening

● Today we're going to look at Mark chapter 8 to find out exactly what it means to be a Christian. We'll see that Jesus says that a Christian is someone who knows who Jesus is, understands why Jesus came and follows Jesus, whatever the cost.

1. A Christian is someone who knows who Jesus is

▶ *A visual aid will help the group follow the pattern of today's talk. Part one should say: "A Christian is someone who knows who Jesus is:"*

● You might be wondering why we're thinking about who Jesus is yet again. After all, Mark tells us the answer right at the beginning of his book. He tells us that Jesus is the "Christ, the Son of God". And we've seen plenty of evidence since then to back that up.

● But Jesus' followers had seen plenty of evidence too – and they still needed help to see who he really is.

▶ *Use the following illustration to help your group think about seeing people in two different ways. Show them the picture (downloadable from www.christianityexplored. org/cy) and ask someone to tell you what they see. If they say "an old woman", ask how many others can see an old woman. Ask if anyone can see anything else. Give them clues if necessary until all, or most of them, can see both the beautiful young woman and the ugly old woman.*

- Jesus' closest friends, the disciples, had been with him for several years. They'd seen and heard amazing things. They'd seen Jesus heal loads of people; stop a storm; control evil spirits and bring a young girl back to life. They'd listened to his teaching about God, and seen for themselves how people responded to his words. They were with him all the time and yet had never seen him do or say anything wrong, cruel or untrue.

- They'd seen and heard all this – but they still didn't see who Jesus really was. Until one day, when at last they began to see the truth:

▶ Read aloud **Mark 8:27-29**.

1a: Jesus is the Christ

- God had opened Peter's eyes so that he could see the truth. Jesus wasn't just a man who could do amazing things. He was the Christ – the rescuing King God had promised to send.

▶ *Illustrate this by explaining that someone was chosen as king by being anointed with oil. Either demonstrate this by holding up a small flask or jug, or simply act out pouring oil from an imaginary flask. Pretend to pour oil onto the head of a boy in your group and explain that this makes him a king, eg: "When I anoint Ryan with oil, it makes him 'King Ryan'". Then explain that the Greek word "Christ" means "the anointed one". So if Jesus is the Christ, it means he is anointed as God's chosen King. (If wanted, you could explain that this is similar to when someone is knighted – they are tapped on the shoulder with a sword, and rise as "Sir whoever".)*

- Peter was right in saying that Jesus is the Christ. He is the King God had promised to send hundreds of years earlier – the King who would rescue his people.

1b: Jesus is the Son of God

- Jesus isn't just the Christ, he's also God's Son. Mark's shown us that Jesus has the power and authority that only God has. We've seen him forgive sins, heal people and control nature. We've seen that he has power over demons, and even over death itself. He has the same power and authority as God – because he is God. Even the demons shouted out that Jesus was the Son of God! (Mark 5:7) (If your group already know the story, you could also mention that God himself calls Jesus his Son at his baptism – Mark 1:11.)

❯ When Peter and the others looked at Jesus, they weren't just seeing a human being – they were seeing God. Like the picture we looked at, which shows both an old and young woman – Jesus was both a man and also God.

▶ *Add the following to your visual aid: "Jesus is the Christ, the Son of God."*

2. A Christian is someone who understands why Jesus came

▶ *Part two of the visual aid should say: "A Christian is someone who understands why Jesus came:"*

❯ You can imagine how excited Peter and the others must have been when they realised that Jesus is the promised King they'd been waiting for. But Jesus had a shock for them:

▶ *Read aloud* **Mark 8:30-31**.

❯ "The Son of Man" is a name Jesus often used when talking about himself. It comes from the Old Testament book of Daniel – from one of the many promises about God sending his chosen King. It says that "one like a son of man" will be king for ever (Daniel 7:13-14). So when Jesus uses the name "The Son of Man", he's confirming that he really is the Christ, God's promised King.

2a: Jesus came to die

❯ But then Jesus said something that would have shocked his followers to the core.

    ❯ He was going to suffer

    ❯ He would be rejected by the religious leaders

    ❯ He would be killed.

❯ He didn't even say it *might* happen – he said it *must* happen.

❯ Peter was stunned. Surely this couldn't be right? Wasn't Jesus the King who was going to rescue them? So Peter dragged Jesus off to have a quiet word.

▶ *Read aloud* **Mark 8:32-33**.

❯ Isn't that a bit harsh? Peter was only saying he didn't want Jesus to die. So why does Jesus call him Satan?

❯ Peter had the wrong kind of king in mind. He wanted Jesus to rule as king in Israel, and to kick out the hated Romans. Jesus calls these ideas "the things of men" – a human king ruling over a physical country.

❯ But Jesus knew that he had come to die. That was how he was going to rescue his people, by giving his life as a ransom for many. That was God's plan – the "things of God", as he calls it. But the devil always wants to spoil God's plans. He would have been delighted if Jesus had chosen to become Peter's kind of king. Peter was saying exactly what Satan wanted.

2b: Jesus came to take the punishment we deserve

◉ Why did "the things of God" mean that Jesus had to die? Because it was the only way to solve the problem of sin; the only way to rescue us from God's judgment. Jesus died in *our* place, taking the punishment *we* deserve. This was the only way we can be forgiven; the only way sinful people can be brought back into a relationship with God.

▣ *Add the following to your visual aid: "Jesus came to die in our place, taking the punishment we deserve."*

3. A Christian is someone who follows Jesus

▣ *Part three of the visual aid should say: "A Christian is someone who follows Jesus:"*

◉ A Christian isn't just someone who knows who Jesus is and why he came – even Satan knows those things. A Christian is someone who follows Jesus, whatever the cost.

▣ *Read aloud* **Mark 8:34**.

▣ *Ask the group: What do you think it means to "deny ourselves"? Listen to their suggestions, then build them in where possible to what you say next. This will help you to add some concrete examples to the explanation of "denying ourselves".*

◉ It doesn't mean denying who we are, or pretending we're something we're not. It means no longer living for ourselves and our own selfish desires. Instead, it means living for Jesus and for others. It means putting Jesus first in every part of our lives. It means Jesus comes first in how we use our time and spend our money. It means we care about what others need, rather than what we want – just as Jesus did.

▣ *Show a picture of a cross, or of someone carrying a cross. Remind your group that the cross was an ancient torture device. The Romans used it as a way of publicly and painfully killing people. In those days, if you saw someone carrying a cross, you knew they were on their way to their own execution.*

◉ Anyone carrying a cross was going to suffer. They would be publicly humiliated; they would be insulted and laughed at; they would be stripped and beaten; and they would die a slow, painful death. So why does Jesus say that anyone who follows him must take up their cross?

◉ If we follow Jesus, we should expect to suffer. We may find that our friends or family laugh at us and try to make us give up living as a Christian. We might find ourselves cut off from people we used to spend time with. If we try to tell people about Jesus, they may refuse to listen and make fun of us for believing in him. And there are plenty of examples in history and today of people who lose their jobs, their families and even their lives for Jesus. (If you want, you could give a modern illustration of Christians facing persecution. Examples can be found at www.barnabasfund.org)

◉ Taking up our cross means being prepared to follow Jesus, whatever the cost.

▣ *Add the following to your visual aid: "A Christian is someone who follows Jesus, whatever the cost."*

- If the cost is going to be so high, why would anyone choose to follow Jesus? He gives us a convincing reason in the next few verses:

▶ *Read aloud* **Mark 8:35-38**.

- Jesus isn't saying that you need to literally die, but that the way to save your life is actually to lose it. If we give our lives to Jesus, he will save them.

- One of the things the resurrection proves is that Jesus is coming back one day, to judge everyone who has ever lived. We don't know when it will be, but we do know he's coming. And when he comes, he'll treat us as we have treated him. If we've rejected him – if we're ashamed of him and his words – he'll be ashamed of us and will reject us.

- But if we give our lives to Jesus, he'll save us. We will know and enjoy God now, as our loving heavenly Father. And we can look forward to eternity with him when we die.

Conclusion
▶ *Refer back to the finished visual aid.*

- So that's what a Christian is:

  - Someone who knows who Jesus is

  - Someone who understands why Jesus came

  - Someone who follows Jesus, whatever the cost.

- Jesus calls each one of us to follow him.

- Some of you may already be sure that you're Christians and that you're living for Jesus. If that's you, I hope this course has helped you grow in your knowledge of Jesus, and think more deeply about what it means to live for him.

- Some of you may feel you don't know enough yet to make a decision about Jesus. If so, I'll give you some suggestions later of ways you can carry on finding out about Jesus.

- But some of you may realise that you're ready to start following Jesus now. If that's you, there will be an opportunity to do that at the end of this session.

DOWNLOAD
The recap (called DOWNLOAD) below appears in the participant's CY Nano Handbook for their reference.

- A Christian is someone who knows who Jesus is: the Son of God, the "Christ", the King who was promised throughout the Old Testament.

- A Christian is someone who understands why Jesus came: he came to die as the only way sinful people can be brought back into a friendship with God.

- A Christian is someone who follows Jesus: Jesus says: "If anyone would come after me, he must deny himself and take up his cross and follow me" (Mark 8:34).

Denying self means no longer living for ourselves but for Jesus and others. Taking up our cross means being prepared to follow him, whatever the cost.

❯ Jesus gives a convincing reason to live like this: "Whoever loses his life for me and for the gospel will save it" (Mark 8:35). If we give our lives to him, he will save them. We will know and enjoy God now, and spend eternity with him when we die.

TALKBACK
▶ *Use the questions below to encourage discussion (they are also printed in the participant's CY Nano Handbook).*

How would you score the following statements? (0 = completely unconvinced; 10 = very sure)

- ☐ **Jesus is God.**
- ☐ **Jesus came to rescue us from our sin.**
- ☐ **Following Jesus means denying ourselves and putting Jesus first, whatever the cost.**

❯ These questions are designed to see how much the group has absorbed about the content of the Christian message during the CY Nano course.

What choices will you make now that you've finished CY Nano? What are you going to do next?

❯ Write down everyone's answer so you can plan a way ahead and pray for them appropriately.

❯ You need gently to encourage people to opt for one of three routes:

1. "I need more time to think." Even if someone thinks that Jesus is definitely not for them, encourage them not to close the door but to keep putting themselves in the place where they will hear about Jesus and spend time with those who follow him. For others, who genuinely do not have enough information or need more time to absorb and think through the gospel message, the same encouragement is appropriate.

2. "I would like to become a Christian." It would be good for anyone who has reached this point to see if they really understand what repentance means.

3. "I know I'm a Christian. I want to live for Jesus in every part of my life, whatever the cost." Any of your group members who are already Christians can be challenged to count the cost of living for Jesus every day. There may be particular areas of their life where they need to repent and to ask the Holy Spirit to help them live wholeheartedly for Jesus.

❯ It may be appropriate to say a prayer of commitment with the whole group – see below. (See page 158 for guidance on how and if to use prayers of commitment.) There is also an alternative prayer which may be more appropriate if some or all of your group are not ready to follow Christ.

CONCLUSION

▶ *As this is the end of the course, expand upon the choices now available to group members. This could include handing out church details or invites to a youth group. Don't forget to follow up with each of the group members (see "After the Course" in Section 1 of this book).*

▶ *Make sure you have answered all of the questions from session 1.*

You could close by saying: Thank you for coming to CY Nano. I really hope you've enjoyed it. If you've become convinced of who Jesus is and what he came to do, and you understand what it will mean to follow him, you may want to echo the following prayer quietly in your own heart:

> **Heavenly Father, I have rebelled against you. I have sinned in my thoughts, my words and my actions. I am sorry for the way I have lived and ask you to forgive me. Thank you so much that Jesus died on the cross so that I could be forgiven. Thank you that Jesus rose again and is ruling as King over everyone and everything. Please send your Holy Spirit so that I can follow Jesus whatever the cost and live with him as King of my life. Amen.**

If you did pray that prayer, let me know – I'd love to help you start living as a Christian.

Note: *Depending on your group, you may find the following prayer helpful instead of or as well as the one above:*

> *Dear God, there are so many questions in my mind, and so many things I am unsure of. Thank you for the time we have spent looking at Mark's Gospel and for the people in this group. Thank you that we now know more about who Jesus is and why he came. Please help me to find answers to my questions, as I learn more about Jesus. And help us to understand the greatness of your love for each one of us in sending your Son Jesus to die for us. Amen.*

▶ *Explain to the group that you want to know what they thought of CY Nano, so that you can do it better next time. Ask them to fill out the FEEDBACK FORM (hand them out). Assure them that their forms will be treated with strict confidence, and not shown to anyone else.*

AFTERWARDS

- ❂ Did any of the group members say they would like to find out more or attend another course? If so, plan how you will follow that up, as well as praying for that person.

- ❂ Thank God for all those who came on the course, and for giving you the privilege of sharing the good news about Jesus with them.

- ❂ Pray for those who have said they need more time to think. Pray that the Holy Spirit will convict them of their need to accept the gift of forgiveness.

- ❂ If any are already Christians, pray that they will grow in their understanding of God's grace and have the courage to talk openly about their faith in Jesus.

CY Study Guide

Before we begin

This section contains the studies to work through over the seven-week *CY* course. It includes all the material in the group member's *CY Handbook*, together with a range of activities, and answers to the questions.

The *CY* course has been written with 15-18s and young adults in mind. The sessions work alongside the *Soul* DVD, and the activities and questions are designed to stretch and challenge older teenagers and young adults.

However, you know your group best. It may be appropriate to choose some activities from the younger *CY Nano* course, which can be found in Section 2 of this Leader's Guide. You may also decide that replacing some or all of the episodes from the *Soul* DVD with talks from the *CY Nano* course will suit your particular group better. We have aimed to keep the material as flexible as possible to allow you to make these adjustments easily if they would help your group.

Christianity is Christ

▶ *Welcome the group and thank them for coming. Introduce yourself if necessary, letting them know that you are there to help and answer any questions they might have.*

▶ *Explain how the session will work and what time it will finish. Let the group know what kinds of things they will be doing, eg:* We'll be doing some warm-up activities to get to know each other a little, having a brief discussion, watching a DVD, and then looking together at a bit of the Bible. There will be plenty of time and opportunity for you to ask any question you want to.

▶ *Explain that no one will be asked to read out loud, pray, or answer any question they don't want to. This group is about trying to look at the answers to the big questions of life in a relaxed way.*

OPTIONAL GROUP ACTIVITY

▶ *If it is appropriate for your group, start the session with an icebreaker activity. You may also want to look at the activities suggested for the younger age group – SIGNATURE BINGO and HOT POTATO on pages 43-44 – they may be appropriate for your group.*

2-MINUTE MIXER
Aim: To get everyone to know each other and to "break the ice".

Equipment: CD/MP3 player; timer; whistle, gong or car horn.

❯ This is essentially "speed dating", but where the aim is to share a few bits of information with each other, so that everyone meets each other.

❯ Tell the group that they must talk to 5 different people for two minutes each, and share the following information with them: Full name (including middle names!); where they were born; their most precious possession; their closest friend; the reason they decided to come to this CY group; an unusual fact about themselves; what is the first thing they would buy if they were given loads of money, etc. Choose a short list of questions that is suitable for your group. You may want to put the questions up on a flipchart or powerpoint slide where people can see them.

Leader's checklist

Have you...

☐ Made it clear to people the time and place where you will meet?

☐ Collected any items needed for the activities?

☐ Enough Bibles or Mark's Gospels for the group?

☐ CY Nano Handbooks and a pen or pencil for each group member?

☐ Set up the Soul DVD ready to play? (Or prepared the optional talk and added any personal illustrations.)

☐ Thought through your answers to each of the questions?

☐ Prayed for each group member and yourself as the leader?

- Play music during this time, and blow a whistle or bang a gong (or just shout) when the 2 minutes is up.

Note: If you have a larger group, you could do this in 1 minute, so that people get to speak to more people. It will create a more energetic activity.

TRUE OR FALSE?
Aim: To get everyone to know each other and to "break the ice".

Equipment: None.

- Ask a group member to give three "facts" about him/herself - two of which are true and one made up.

- The rest of the group then votes on which "fact" is the made-up one.

- Repeat until every group member has had a turn at giving their three "facts".

Note: Do this as one group if possible, to help you get to know each other - but if you have a larger group, divide into small groups with a leader in each one to run the game.

▶ *If neither of these activities will work for your group or for yourself, there are more ideas online at www.christianityexplored.org/cy. Or feel free not to use any!*

EXPLORE
▶ *Give a CY Handbook to each participant. Ask them to turn to page 4 and to write down their answer to this question:*

> **If you could ask God one question, and you knew it would be answered, what would it be?**

▶ *Ask the group to share their answers. Note down what they are so that you can deal with them at some point during the course. Don't attempt to answer all the questions at this time, but do acknowledge every question and assure participants that they will be covered during CY. (Some questions will be answered by the talks and some – like questions about suffering – are best dealt with after the talks on the cross / grace.) However, you may want to answer one or two short questions at this point, if they are simple to deal with and not contentious. You might also want to write your own question and share it with the group. **Note:** If your group members would be embarrassed to say their questions, ask them to write them on a piece of paper and put them in a "question box". You can then collect all the questions from the box and read them to the group.*

▶ *Reassure the group that the questions they are asking are perfectly normal – and they are questions that many people have about life and God. You may even say that this is a question that you have struggled with. This is to help people see that the things they may feel very intensely about are things that others struggle to understand too.*

▶ *Either here, or after the talk, the group may ask questions on science/evolution/ creation. Make sure you plan a time to talk about this – probably during a later session, using the notes on page 206. It may be enough at this point to say that the course is not making any particular point about evolution or creation. We're simply showing that we are either the result of an accident or we have been made by someone – and that this makes a difference to how we see "the meaning of life".*

GROUP ACTIVITY: POSTER

▶ *Give the group one large piece of paper and some pens. Ask them to draw a poster of things that come into their minds when they think of Christianity. For example, they might draw a large cathedral or church. If some of the group prefer not to draw, they can write single words on the poster instead.*

Note: Leaders need to allow the group to draw what they want. If they want to draw something that is theologically problematic, allow them to do it because there will be an opportunity later to correct misunderstandings.

Note: It is important to do this activity as it is referred to in the study questions.

OPTIONAL GROUP ACTIVITY: FOOTBALL PITCH

▶ *Give the group one large piece of paper and some pens. On it draw a football pitch or soccer field with areas marked like the diagram below: supporters, opposition, entrance, injury bench etc. Ask participants to mark with a cross where they think they are at the moment, ie: a player would be someone who thinks they are already a Christian; coming in the entrance would be someone who doesn't know much about the Christian faith, and is just starting to look it over; injured – has been a Christian, but is now not sure; opposition – hostile to Christianity for some reason; supporters – have always been to church (from a Christian family perhaps) but starting to ask if this is the team they want to support for the rest of their lives.*

Explain that this is to help them, not for others to judge them. Allow people to think it over and put a cross where they think they are, and give them the chance to explain why they put their mark where they did. **Do not force anyone to put a mark if they don't want to.**

Note: This activity is optional. If you think it will be unhelpful for your group, or you are concerned that it may "pigeonhole" them right at the beginning of the course, then don't use it.

You can download a sheet with this illustration on it at www.christianityexplored.org/cy.

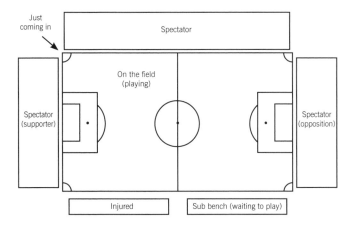

▶ *Give each person a Bible. Show them where they can find Mark's Gospel. Explain how chapters and verses work.*

▶ *Ask everyone to turn to* **Mark 1:1**. (**Note:** *The questions and quotes in CY are based on the NIV.)*

▶ *One of the leaders should read* **Mark 1:1** *aloud; then the group should work through the questions below. The answers are given here for your reference.*

> **What does Mark say Christianity is all about in the first sentence of his book?**

- ❯ He says that it is "good news". (Explain that the word "gospel" means "good news".)

- ❯ He says it's about Jesus.

- ❯ He says it's about Jesus being the Son of God. (*see note on this below)

Note: *Some eagle-eyed participants may notice a footnote in the NIV that says: "Some ancient manuscripts do not have the words 'the Son of God'", and ask you about it. This may, in turn, raise all kinds of issues about the reliability of the Bible, and the trustworthiness of Mark. If this is an issue for your group, or for an individual, plan to include some input on the reliability of the Bible. See notes on page 203.*

> **How is that different from some of the pictures we've drawn?**

This question is designed to tackle some of the common misconceptions about the Christian faith that may have come up in the poster-drawing exercise.

- ❯ He says that it is "good news". In other words – it's not bad news; it's great, brilliant and exciting news - far from boring! If you think Christianity is boring, then you've not really understood what it's all about.

- ❯ He says it's about Jesus. It's not about buildings, or services, or "religion" – it's about a man who lived and walked and breathed in history, called Jesus.

- ❯ He says it's about Jesus being the Son of God. It's about God making himself known to us through Jesus.

DVD PRESENTATION
▶ *Watch Episode 1 of the Soul DVD, or deliver Talk 1 using the notes on page 46. The notes for this talk can also be downloaded from www.christianityexplored.org/cy to enable you to adapt them for your group and add your own illustrations.*

▶ *There is a recap (called DOWNLOAD) in the participant's CY Handbook for their reference. Encourage people to write notes on the Download page as they listen to the talk. The recap is also printed below.*

DOWNLOAD
- ❯ Christianity is not about rules or ceremonies. It's all about Jesus Christ.

- ❯ If we're here by chance, we have no real significance or value. But God created us - so we matter enormously.

- We all face death sooner or later. Since we all have to die, what's the point of living?

- The Bible says we don't really start living until we know the one who made us, and live as he made us to live.

- But how can we get to know God? We need him to reveal himself to us. Mark says he's done that for us by sending Jesus Christ. If we want to know what God is like, we must look at Jesus.

- That's why "the gospel about Jesus Christ" is good news.

TALKBACK

▶ *Use the questions below to encourage discussion (they are also printed in the participant's CY Handbook).*

▶ *Remember that this is the first session, and the aim here is not to explain the whole gospel, challenge them to become Christians, or to start an argument about what they currently believe. It is simply to open up the themes that will be covered in subsequent weeks.*

▶ *Be careful that TALKBACK does not run over time. It is much better to stop a good discussion, leaving them hungry for more, than to talk everything out in detail with the risk of boring some of the group, or putting them off coming back next time.*

If you asked a group of people in the street: "What is the point of life?", what kind of answers would you get?

- Answers might include: making lots of money; having a good time; having good friends; finding love.

- You might ask them why they think different people think different things are important.

- The aim here is not to criticize these views, but to get the group thinking about the meaning of life. There is no pressing need to comment on them now, unless the discussion naturally heads that way.

What do most people think about God and Christianity? Why do you think that is?

- This is to recap the EXPLORE questions, without getting too personal. Answers may include: boring, irrelevant, outdated, full of rules etc.

- Explain that churches can very easily forget that Christianity is all about Jesus – and the resulting religion can become any or all of those things. But this is not real Christianity.

- If necessary, sympathize with anyone in the group who may have had a bad experience of religion – an unhelpful minister, boring services etc.

What about Jesus? Do people think he matters? What do *you* think?

- At this stage don't press anyone to give an answer for what they think, but if they do, it may be appropriate to ask them why.

❷ Remind them that, according to Mark 1:1, Jesus is "good news".

CONCLUSION

Finish by encouraging your group members to come back next time. Tell them: We've seen that Mark says that Christianity is all about one man, Jesus. Next time we'll find out about some of the things Jesus did and said, and why Mark says that Jesus is "good news".

AFTERWARDS

❷ Write down the questions that people have come up with, so that you can be sure to address them in the coming weeks. It may be helpful at this point to prepare a plan of which question you deal with each session.

❷ Think about the people who came. Make a list so that you can pray for them.

❷ Think about what contact you may want to make during the week to encourage them to come next time.

Identity

▶ *Welcome the group and thank them for coming.*

▶ *Recap on the previous session:*
Last time we saw that Christianity is not about beautiful buildings and boring services – it is all about Jesus Christ.

Remember Mark chapter 1, verse 1? "The beginning of the gospel about Jesus Christ, the Son of God."

But what was Jesus really like? Well, that's what we're going to look at this time.

GROUP ACTIVITY

▶ *If it is appropriate for your group, start the session with one of the activities below. You may also want to look at the activities suggested for the younger age group – GUESS WHO? and FIVE FACTS on pages 51-52 – they may be appropriate for your group.*

GUESS WHO I AM?

Aim: To show that a person's qualities reveal their true identity.

Equipment: Blank stickers.

● Write the names of famous and well-known people on stickers. As people arrive, put one on each person's back (or forehead).

● Group members must then find out who they are, by asking questions of fellow group members, who may only answer "yes" or "no". When they have guessed their identity, they can either come to you for another, or just help others to discover their identities.

At the end of the activity, say to participants: "Once you get all the facts about a person, you can tell who they are. This week we're going to get some facts from Mark's biography of Jesus so we can find out who Jesus really is."

Leader's checklist

Have you...

☐ Reminded group members where and when you will meet (eg: by email or text message)?

☐ Collected any items needed for the activities?

☐ Enough Bibles or Mark's Gospels for the group?

☐ CY Handbooks and a pen or pencil for each group member?

☐ Set up the Soul DVD ready to play? (Or prepared the optional talk and added any personal illustrations.)

☐ Thought through your answers to each of the questions?

☐ Prayed for each group member and yourself as the leader?

DARK SECRETS

Aim: To show that there is more to people than it may seem at first. To get to know group members better.

Suitable for: Groups where people know each other well.

- ❯ Collect interesting facts about people who are in the group – leaders as well as group members. And/or collect some baby photographs of people in the room. You will need to plan this well in advance.

- ❯ Show each photo and/or read out the interesting fact about that person. Then get the group to suggest who in the group they think it might be. When people have voted with a show of hands, ask the real person to stand up, or raise their hand.

At the end of the activity, say to participants: "People can often surprise you! You may think they are one thing, but the truth is different. This week we're going to look at what Jesus did and said in Mark's Gospel. You may discover that he is very different from what you thought!"

EXPLORE

▶ *Hand a CY Handbook to each participant. Ask them to turn to page 8 and to write down their answer to this question:*

> **Think of your best friend. What do you really like about them?**

- ❯ *Ask a few participants to share their answers. Then point out:* Isn't it interesting that most of you wrote down things about your friend's character and how they behave, rather than commenting on the way they look? It's those things that make our friends important to us.

- ❯ Do you know that we don't actually have a physical description of Jesus? But we do know a lot about his character and many of the things he did, and we're going to look at that today. Because those qualities tell us some important things about him.

▶ *Ask everyone to turn to* **Mark 2:1–12**.

▶ *Ask someone to read the passage aloud and then work through the questions below with the group.*

> **Why is the house full at the start of this passage? (Look at Mark 1:45 for clues.)**

- ❯ People wanted to come and meet Jesus.

- ❯ He already had a good reputation because he had healed the sick and because his teaching was worth hearing.

> **Imagine you're in the room. How would you have reacted to Jesus saying: "Son, your sins are forgiven"? (See verse 5.)**
> **Why do you think he said it?**

- The man's greatest need appears to be that he should be healed physically.

- However, Jesus knows that the man's even greater need is that he should have his sins forgiven and so he deals with this need first.

- We probably would have only seen the man's physical need. But Jesus saw a deeper need. Jesus knew that the man's sins were more damaging than his disability.

Follow-up question: What do you think "sin" is? Or: What is the difference between "sin" and "sins"?

- Sins are individual things we do wrong, like lying or being unkind. "Sin" is our attitude which means we think it is OK to do sins. It is the difference between the disease and the symptoms. Sin is the disease. Sins are the symptoms.

Note: *Sin is covered in more detail in Session 3 (Mission). But in the meantime it might be helpful to think of sin like this: "Shove off God. I'm in charge, Not you!". Point out that sin isn't just the wrong stuff we do, it's also our attitude to God. Sin is a problem because it cuts us off from God and stops us from knowing him.*

Why do the religious leaders react so strongly when Jesus forgives the man's sin? (See verse 7.) Do you think their response is right?

- They know that sins can only be forgiven by God and so for Jesus to forgive sins is to claim that he is God.

- Because sin offends God, only God can forgive it.

- The religious leaders are partly right, in that only God can forgive sin. But they are also wrong because Jesus is not blaspheming (lying about God): he really is God.

Optional follow-up question: Notice that Jesus is in conflict with the religious leaders of his day! They are suspicious of him. He challenges them. What does this tell us about how we should view anyone who claims to "know the truth about God"?

- Any religious leader can be wrong! We need to check out where they got their information from, and what their authority is.

Note: *Don't let this question become a red herring! If you're short of time, or think it will be a distraction from focusing on Jesus, don't ask it.*

Jesus heals the man so that he can walk. What is the real reason Jesus healed him? (Look at verse 10 for a clue.)

- Jesus does this to prove that he really does have authority to forgive sins.

- No one can see that the man's sins have really been forgiven, because it is the man's relationship with God that has been changed. So Jesus does something visibly miraculous to show that he really does have the power to forgive him.

- Anyone can claim to forgive another person's sins, but they won't be able to prove they have. Jesus was able to prove he had the authority and ability to forgive sins.

Optional follow-up question: What happens if someone does not forgive us?

Why is it so important to be forgiven by God?

- If there is no forgiveness, then there is no possibility of being friends again. If we have sinned against God, God must forgive us in order for us to have a right relationship with him.

DVD PRESENTATION

▶ *Watch Episode 2 of the Soul DVD, or deliver Talk 2 using the notes on page 54. The notes for this talk can also be downloaded from www.christianityexplored.org/cy to enable you to adapt them for your group and add your own illustrations.*

▶ *There is a recap (called DOWNLOAD) in the participant's CY Handbook for their reference. Encourage people to write notes on the Download page as they listen to the talk. The recap is also printed below.*

DOWNLOAD

- Mark 1:1 says that Jesus is the "Christ" – which means the chosen one of God, God's promised King – and "the Son of God". Mark then shows us that:

- Jesus can forgive sins – Mark 2:1-10

- Jesus has power to heal – Mark 2:11-12

- Jesus has power over nature – Mark 4:35-41

- Jesus has power over demons – Mark 5:1-17

- Jesus has power over death – Mark 5:35-42

TALKBACK

▶ *Use the questions below to encourage discussion (they are also printed in the participant's CY Handbook).*

> **Which of the events Mark tells us about would you have found most amazing or scary? Why?**

- This question is designed to get the group talking about the actual events that have been described by Mark and explained by the talk.

- As they are talking about it, try to get them to see the difference between the amazement they would experience seeing a magic trick, say, and the disturbing shock of seeing the things that Jesus did – disturbing because of what they reveal about Jesus.

- You might like to link back to the opening activity:
  - "In our opening activity we saw that a person's qualities reveal their true identity. What would you have concluded about who Jesus was if you were there and saw all the amazing things he was doing?"

What do *you* think of Jesus?

- This is a more direct question, although it is okay for people to reserve judgement at this stage by saying: "I'm not sure yet". As the weeks go on, the evidence will become more compelling.

- It may be appropriate at this stage to show why it is simply not right to say that Jesus was "just" a good man, or a teacher, or a religious leader – he must either be a fake, a lunatic or exactly who he claims to be.

Optional follow-up question: What information was your view of Jesus based on? Why do you trust that source? What are good reasons for doubting it?

- People often accept a version of Jesus from half-heard popular versions of the stories about Jesus rather than the actual accounts of his life and teaching. Young people often grow up accepting their parents' faith – or lack of it. People from Christian homes will need challenging to work it out for themselves. Young people with an uncritical acceptance of atheism, or some other view, will need challenging to question why they believe what they believe. Always go back to the question: "What evidence is that view based on?"

▶ *If you have time, now is the moment to answer another of the questions that were asked in the first week's EXPLORE: "If you could ask God one question, and you knew it would be answered, what would it be?" See page 191 for guidance notes on common questions.*

▶ *Be careful that you do not over-run on time. It's always better to leave them wanting more and eager to return next time.*

CONCLUSION
Finish by encouraging your group members to come back next time. Tell them: We've seen some of the remarkable things Jesus did and said – that show us that he is who Mark says he is: the Christ, the Son of God. Next time we're going to explore further what Jesus said about himself.

AFTERWARDS
- Did any of the group members ask a question or make a comment that you could follow up? If so, plan how you will do that, as well as praying for that person.

- Thank God for those who came back this session, and pray that he will open their hearts to the truth about Jesus.

- Was anyone missing who came last time? Plan to contact them during the week to ask how they are and encourage them to come next time.

✗ **READ MARK 12:28–31**

What does it mean to love God with all your heart, with all your soul, with all your mind and with all your strength?

What does it mean to love your neighbour as yourself?

up to these two
down?

13

explore

3 Mission

What do you think is the biggest problem facing the world?

From last time's session, what does Jesus think is the biggest problem facing the world?

12

Mission

▶ *Welcome the group and thank them for coming.*

▶ *Recap on the previous session:*
Last time we saw from Mark's Gospel some of the amazing things Jesus did and said. We saw that Jesus claimed to be able to forgive sins; that he had power to heal; and that he had power over nature, demons and even death. We saw that Jesus has the same power as God – because Jesus is God.

This time we are going to dig deeper and look at what Jesus said about himself and about why he came – his mission.

GROUP ACTIVITY

▶ *If it is appropriate for your group, start the session with one of the activities below. You may also want to look at the activities suggested for the younger age group – WRONG SKETCH and WRONG EQUIPMENT on pages 61-62 – they may be appropriate for your group.*

HIGH RISE

Aim: To explore how we judge what makes someone better than someone else.

Equipment: A flipchart with a drawing of a high-rise tower block as on the next page; cards with names written on; sticky tape or blu-tac. Cards should have names of prominent "do-gooders" on as well as notorious "do-badders"! For example: pop stars who raise money for charity, celebrities with drug problems etc. There should also be cards with generic groups like "members of the Mafia", "Child murderers", "Rapists", "Politicians", "Doctors", "Nurses", "Mothers", "Fathers", "Pickpockets", "Bank Managers", "Financial traders" etc.

❯ Say that in this high-rise building, the better people get to live on a higher floor. The worst people go down below in the basement. The very best live in the penthouse.

❯ Hand out the cards randomly to group members, who should stick their card on the high-rise floor they think that person or group should live on. As people put the cards up, ask them why they put them there.

Leader's checklist

Have you...

☐ Reminded the group about the next meeting?

☐ Collected any items needed for the activities?

☐ Enough Bibles or Mark's Gospels for the group?

☐ CY Handbooks and pens for each group member?

☐ Set up the Soul DVD ready to play? (Or prepared the optional talk and added any personal illustrations.)

☐ Thought through your answers to the questions?

☐ Invitations to the "Inside Track" weekend/day away?

☐ Prayed for each group member and yourself as the leader?

❷ As an add-on, you could finish by giving each person a card simply saying "Me".

At the end of the activity, say to participants: "Today we're going to look at a difficult subject which might be uncomfortable for us. We judge each other by our standards, but God judges us by his standards. We're going to look at what God thinks we are like." (You might return to this later in the session – see below.)

HIGH RISE

COLA ILLUSTRATION
Aim: To show that sin is a problem of the heart – inside us.

Equipment: 2 cola bottles, one new, one that's been rolled in mud – both filled with cold coffee mixed with salt (so that it looks like cola but tastes disgusting!); two plastic cups – or enough cups for the whole group.

❷ Either choose two volunteers to taste what's in the two bottles, or give everyone in the group a plastic cup each and let them to choose which bottle they want to taste.

❷ After the "cola" has been tasted, explain that people are like that. Some look nice on the outside, some don't – but all of us are wrong on the inside.

❷ Then clean the outside of both bottles with water and a cloth, and ask who would like another taste now that both bottles are clean.

- Explain that people sometimes try to do the same thing – they try to clean themselves up on the outside. But we'll see today that sin comes from inside us, so making ourselves look nice or good can't solve the problem of sin.

At the end of the activity, say to participants: "Today we're going to have a look at what Jesus said about sin, and how his mission was to make it possible for us to be made clean on the inside."

Note: There is an example of how this cola illustration can be developed further at www.christianityexplored.org/cy.

EXPLORE

▶ *Hand a CY Handbook to each participant. Ask them to turn to page 12 and to write down their answer to this question:*

What do you think is the biggest problem facing the world?

- Ask the group to share their answers and discuss as appropriate. People may come up with big global issues (global warming, wars), closer-to-home social issues (unemployment, crime), or personal issues (lack of meaning and purpose in life, broken relationships). If the group has missed one of these categories, suggest it to them.

- When possible problems are suggested, see if other members of the group agree and if not, ask them why not.

Note: *For research on this, or even to do "live" with a projector – type "World's biggest problem" into Google or YouTube and see what information or illustration you can find.*

From last time's CY, what does Jesus think is the biggest problem facing the world?

- Get the answer from the group.

- In Mark 2:1–12 we saw that Jesus did not deal first with the man's paralysis but with his sin. According to Jesus, the biggest problem facing the world is our sin. (You may want to quickly recap the story of the paralysed man, especially if any of your group missed last week's session.)

- Recap what was said last week about sin, eg: **S**hove off God. **I**'m in charge, **N**ot you! Sin isn't just the wrong stuff we do; it's also our attitude to God.

Optional follow-up question: Can you see how sin might be the root of all the other things that we mentioned as the biggest problems?

- Sin is selfish concern. It underlies the vast majority of issues people raise about poverty, wealth, ecology and war. But Jesus' greater concern is not the effects of sin we experience now, which are bad enough, but the way sin has destroyed our relationship with God, and the eternal effects of that.

▶ *Ask everyone to turn to **Mark 12:28–31**.*

▶ *Ask someone to read the passage aloud and then work through the questions below with the group.*

What does it mean to love God with all your heart, with all your soul, with all your mind and with all your strength?

❯ This means that we put God first in our lives. No one and nothing else can take God's place.

❯ You might need to explain what we mean by "love". Some may suggest that you can't choose who you love or even that you cannot control your feelings at all. We're talking here about love that is more about what you *do* than how you *feel*.

Note: *It may be helpful to give a concrete example of what that means by turning to the first part of the ten commandments (Exodus 20:1–11). For example, you could refer your group to Exodus 20:7 and talk about whether they have ever misused God's name.*

Optional follow-up question: Can you force someone to be loving?

❯ People may react against the notion that God commands us to love him and others.

❯ Explain that love for God and others comes out of a relationship with God where we want to please Him, because we have understood how wise, kind, loving, forgiving and generous He is.

What does it mean to love your neighbour as yourself?

❯ It means that we should treat other people as we would like to be treated ourselves. It might be helpful to point out that there are two parts to this rule: love *others* and love *self*. This may help anyone who struggles with self-hate.

Note: *It may be helpful to give a concrete example of what that means by turning to the second part of the ten commandments (Exodus 20:12–17). For example, you could refer your group to Exodus 20:16 and talk about whether they have ever lied to someone.*

❯ Notice that Jesus is not only interested in the way we seem outwardly, but also the way we are deep down, in our hearts and minds. (Older groups may find it helpful to see how Jesus applies Old Testament laws in this way in Matthew 5:21–22 and Matthew 5:27–28.)

How good do you think you are at living up to these two commands? Where do you especially mess up?

❯ This question is designed to help the group see that everyone falls short of these two commands – the two most important of God's commands according to Jesus. This means we're **all** sinners.

❯ You could get the discussion going by admitting that you yourself find it impossible always to obey these two commands. (It may be appropriate to be specific!) Or you could list how the group members like to be treated by others; then go back over the list asking if that is how they always treat everyone else.

DVD PRESENTATION

❯ *Watch Episode 3 of the Soul DVD, or deliver Talk 3 using the notes on page 64. The notes for this talk can also be downloaded from www.christianityexplored.org/cy to enable you to adapt them for your group and add your own illustrations.*

▶ *There is a recap (called DOWNLOAD) in the group member's CY Handbook for their reference. Encourage people to write notes on the Download page as they watch the DVD or listen to the talk. The recap is also printed below.*

DOWNLOAD

- ❯ Jesus came to deal with our biggest problem: our sin (Mark 2:17).

- ❯ Each and every one of us rebels against our loving Creator. That rebellion is what the Bible calls "sin".

- ❯ Sin is a serious problem that will lead us to hell. If we continue to reject God, then he will respond to that decision – and reject us.

- ❯ Only Jesus can rescue us from the problem of sin. Jesus came to rescue rebels.

TALKBACK

▶ *Use the questions below to encourage discussion (they are also printed in the participant's CY Handbook).*

What are some of the reasons people give for why Jesus came?

- ❯ This is a recap on discussions from the last two sessions about Jesus' **identity** (who he is) and **mission** (why he came). Answers might include: "to teach", "to show us love", "to show us how to live".

Do you think sin is a problem? Why or why not?

- ❯ Think about the problems that you have with friends, or about big problems in the world… the root cause is sin.

- ❯ Some group members may not recognize that sin is a problem for them. The next question should help.

How would you feel if all your thoughts, words and actions were on display for everyone to see?

- ❯ The aim here is to help them understand that sin is a problem for them personally.

- ❯ Our sin is a problem: to others (who are hurt by and have to deal with our selfish behaviour); and, most importantly, to God (who will rightly judge us for how we have lived.)

- ❯ In other words, we all break the two most important commands: we all fail to love God and our neighbour as we should.

Follow-up question: Why do we find it so difficult to admit that we fail to live rightly? Why do we pretend we are better than we are?

- ❯ This is what sin does to us as well! We know what we should be, but cover up our failure because we do not dare to admit to ourselves what we are really like inside.

▶ If you used HIGH RISE as a starter activity, now might be the time to go back to it and say: "As we saw when we put names on the high-rise tower block, we judge each other by our standards, but God judges us by his standards. When we compare each other, most of us think we are not too bad. But God sees us as we really are and says that we are all sinners."

▶ Give out invitations to the "Inside Track" weekend/day away, and explain that this will be happening after week 6 of the CY course. See Section 4 on page 161 for details of the "Inside Track" weekend/day way.

▶ If you have time, now is the moment to answer another of the questions that were asked in the first week's EXPLORE: "If you could ask God one question, and you knew it would be answered, what would it be?"

▶ Be careful that you do not over-run on time. It's always better to leave them wanting more and eager to return next time.

CONCLUSION

Finish by encouraging your group members to come back next week. Tell them: We've seen why sin is such a huge problem, and that Jesus came to rescue rebels. If sin is the biggest problem we all face, then surely the answer to that problem would be the best and most important news ever. Come back next time to hear it.

AFTERWARDS

- Did any of the group members ask a question or make a comment that you could follow up? If so, plan how you will do that, as well as praying for that person.

- Pray that this week the Holy Spirit would do his work of convicting group members that they are sinners under the judgment of God.

- Thank God for those who came back this session, and pray that he will open their hearts to the truth about Jesus.

- Was anyone missing who came last time? Plan to contact them during the week to ask how they are and encourage them to next time.

Cross

▶ *Welcome the group and thank them for coming.*

▶ *Recap on the previous session:*
Last time we saw that Jesus came to deal with our biggest problem: the fact that we are sinners. We all sin; we all miss the mark; we all rebel against our loving Creator. We also saw that sin is a serious problem because it leads us to hell – to being separated from God for ever.

At the heart of the Christian message is the cross. The cross is the universal symbol for Christianity. We're going to look in this session at how the death of Jesus on a cross is connected with the problem of sin.

GROUP ACTIVITY

▶ *If it is appropriate for your group, start the session with one of the activities below. You may also want to look at the activities suggested for the younger age group – CELEBRITY PAIRS and RACE FOR THE RANSOM on pages 69-70 – they may be appropriate for your group.*

SALT AND PEPPER

Aim: To show that certain things go together.

Equipment: Post-it notes.

- ❱ Write out the two halves of a matching pair on separate sticky notes.

- ❱ Repeat for each matching pair until you have enough for the whole group – several times over if you're going to play more than one round.

- ❱ Try to match the pairs you use to the type of group you have, so for example, if you are running CY in a college, you could have study subjects matched with the teachers. If you are running it with a group of sports-mad teenage boys, then use managers or star players with the team they play for. Try to be varied in the categories, eg:

  - ❱ Foods – eg: Fish and Chips; Salt and Pepper; Hot dogs and Mustard

  - ❱ People – eg: celebrity couples, royalty

Leader's checklist

Have you...

- ☐ Reminded the group about the next meeting?

- ☐ Collected any items needed for the activities?

- ☐ Enough Bibles or Mark's Gospels for the group?

- ☐ CY Handbooks and pens for each group member?

- ☐ Set up the Soul DVD ready to play? (Or prepared the optional talk and added any personal illustrations.)

- ☐ Thought through your answers to the questions?

- ☐ Spare invitations to the "Inside Track" weekend/ day away?

- ☐ Prayed for each group member and yourself as the leader?

- History – eg: Henry VIII and Anne Boleyn; Bonnie and Clyde; David and Goliath

- Entertainment – eg: Bart and Lisa (Simpson); Tom and Jerry; Kirk and Spock

- Put notes at random on people's backs – they have to find out who they are and discover their partner by only asking questions that can return the answers "yes", "no" and "not relevant".

- You could play a couple of rounds of this game. If it would work for your group, for the final round you could give the paired-off people another pair, and get them to act it out for the whole group to guess (celebrity pairs charades!).

At the end of the activity, say to participants: "Some things form natural pairs. The cross is naturally associated with Christianity or Jesus. Today we're going to look at why the cross is so central to Christianity."

COME ON DOWN!

Aim: To set up the idea of what something is worth.

Equipment: Some household objects.

- This is basically a version of the old TV game show *The Price is Right*. Choose three contestants and stand them before three household objects (A toaster, an expensive handbag, (a model of) a sports car, for example).

- Contestants have to guess what the price of each is – the nearest to the real answer wins. Encourage the "audience" to shout out their suggestions to the participants.

Note: *You could also use pictures from a catalogue or online store - that way you will have easy access to the current prices.*

Alternatives: You could also have some very ordinary objects which mean very little to everyone else but have a special, sentimental value to one of the contestants. Eg: a wedding ring, something that belonged to a long-gone relative etc.

At the end of the activity, say to participants: "We've been thinking about what things are worth. Tonight we will be asking the question – what is a person worth to God?"

EXPLORE

▶ *Hand a CY Handbook to each participant. Ask them to turn to page 16 and to write down their answer to this question:*

> **Imagine you know how and when you will die. How would it make you feel? What would it make you do?**

- This is a question to get people talking. There are no wrong answers, so try to avoid making value judgements on their suggestions.

- Most people might feel terrible knowing when and how they will die. It might make you desperate to try and avoid it. Or else you could go mad, do nothing or perhaps "eat, drink and be merry". Some people might devote the remaining time to helping others.

Note: *Be aware that this question may be a particularly emotive issue for some of your group – especially if they have had a friend or family member die recently. Be extra* *vigilant for anyone who is troubled by this question, and make sure that you set an appropriate tone for the discussion. You should also offer comfort and support to anyone who is struggling with this issue.*

▶ *Ask everyone to turn to* **Mark 8:27-33**.

▶ *Ask someone to read the passage aloud and then work through the questions below with the group.*

What does Peter realize in verse 29?

- Peter realizes that Jesus is the Christ – which means "the anointed one", God's chosen King.

- This is the first time that Peter sees this. This is pretty amazing, considering that he had been around Jesus all the time he was doing miracles, teaching and raising the dead.

Why would Jesus' words in verse 31 surprise Peter?

- It would be surprising to hear that God's King was going to die.

- If it would be helpful to your group, you may want to explain the historical setting. Peter was living in an occupied country, under the rule of the hated Romans. The Jews had been waiting for hundreds of years for God to send the promised Messiah/ Christ. They knew the Messiah would be a rescuing King, so hoped that he would rescue them from the tyranny of the Romans.

Optional follow-up question: What surprises you about what Jesus says?

- It is very detailed and specific.

- All the people who should welcome the Messiah will reject him.

- Jesus speaks plainly about it – he doesn't try to hide it from anyone. If I were talking about something like this, I would do it in hushed tones, and cautiously. Jesus seems extremely confident in both the facts of what will happen, and in accepting what it means for him.

Why does Jesus confront Peter in verse 33?

- Peter is rebuked because he does not consider the "things of God" – in other words, he is looking at Jesus' kingship from a human point of view, not God's point of view. He has realized who Jesus is, but he has not understood that Jesus' mission is to come and die.

Follow-up question: Why does Jesus call Peter "Satan" (the devil)?

- Satan (the name means "accuser" or "adversary") is never very far from Jesus. In Mark, we have already read about how Jesus has freed people suffering from demons (evil spirits), and about how he was tempted by Satan in the wilderness (Mark 1:12-13). Satan wants to stop Jesus carrying out his mission, which will be achieved not by military command, but by dying on the cross as our ransom. Jesus sees that Peter's challenge to him is inspired by the devil – and rejects it.

Note: This opens up a difficult area. Peter was not "controlled" by Satan, in the same way as some of the demon-possessed people were. But he was expressing Satan's thoughts and words.

> **When Jesus died on the cross, was it unexpected? (Look at Mark 9:31 and Mark 10:33–34 for clues.)**

- ❯ The disciples were shocked, but it wasn't unexpected – Jesus had taught his disciples repeatedly about the way he would die.

DVD PRESENTATION

▶ *Watch Episode 4 of the Soul DVD, or deliver Talk 4 using the notes on page 72. The notes for this talk can also be downloaded from www.christianityexplored.org/cy to enable you to adapt them for your group and add your own illustrations.*

▶ *There is a recap (called DOWNLOAD) in the group member's CY Handbook for their reference. Encourage people to write notes on the Download page as they watch the DVD or listen to the talk. The recap is also printed below.*

DOWNLOAD

- ❯ Jesus knew when he was going to die. His death wasn't an accident - it was planned.

- ❯ Jesus' death is the only way we can be saved from our sin. It is the way Jesus rescues us, as "a ransom for many" (Mark 10:45).

- ❯ When Jesus died, he was willingly taking the punishment for *our* sin. He was punished in *our* place, so that *we* can be rescued.

- ❯ Jesus' death makes it possible for us to be accepted by God and enjoy a relationship with him.

- ❯ People have different reactions to Jesus' death: Pontius Pilate goes with the crowd; the soldiers are wrapped up in themselves; the religious leaders think they don't need Jesus; the Roman centurion gets it right, when he says that Jesus is "the Son of God".

TALKBACK

▶ *Use the questions below to encourage discussion (they are also printed in the participant's CY Handbook).*

> **How would you feel if someone else deliberately took the punishment for something serious you had done wrong?**

- ❯ This could bring out a number of differing reactions:
  - ❯ Glad. The other person is a sucker for taking the blame.
  - ❯ Guilty. I should have been punished instead.
  - ❯ Bad. For the person who suffered.
  - ❯ Grateful. Thankful for the person who took your punishment.

- Or any mixture of the above.

- You could follow up with: "What if it is a really bad punishment – not just being told off by a teacher, but actually going to prison?" The question is designed to open up a discussion about guilt, responsibility etc, so there is no need to make any comment about the replies.

Why do you think Jesus' death on the cross is so important to Christians?

Note: *This is an opportunity for you as a leader to express personally what the cross means to you.*

- Because the cross is where our sin (our biggest problem) was dealt with.

- At the cross Jesus took the punishment we deserve. It should have been me dying there, but he died in my place.

- If it weren't for the cross, no one could be forgiven! No one could be acceptable to God!

Note: *These answers concentrate on the way the cross deals with the penalty of sin in the future. But the cross also does much more than this. It breaks the power of sin in the present (we can now resist its influence in our lives), and one day will also save us from the presence of sin (we will live forever with Christ in the new creation free from its influence entirely).*

Which of the reactions to Jesus' death is most like your reaction?

- Some people might not want to answer this in front of others. You could perhaps ask them to underline the one in DOWNLOAD that refers best to them – or start by asking them which reaction they think most of their friends would relate to.

Note: *The differing reactions to Jesus' death are an ideal way of talking about what might influence someone's decision to become a Christian. Young people are often very influenced by the crowd mentality – not wanting to appear as if they are different from the crowd. Others are very wrapped up in their own problems, ideas and thoughts – and do not want to change. It may help group members if you share your own testimony, where it touches on how you struggled with these things. In the end, if people are convinced that the Christian message is true, then they will need to overcome these pressures on them to ignore the gospel.*

▸ *If you have time, now is the moment to answer another of the questions that were asked in the first week's EXPLORE: "If you could ask God one question, and you knew it would be answered, what would it be?"*

▸ *Remind the group about the "Inside Track" weekend/day away, and give out invitations to any who were missing last week or have lost theirs.*

▸ *Be careful that you do not over-run on time. It's always better to leave them wanting more and eager to return next time.*

CONCLUSION

Finish by encouraging your group members to come back next time. Tell them: We've seen why the death of Jesus is so important to Christians. But what happened next? After Good Friday comes Easter Day. The Bible tells us that Jesus came back to life again – but would it matter if he hadn't? Next time we'll see why it matters that Jesus came back from the dead.

AFTERWARDS

- ❯ Did any of the group members ask a question or make a comment that you could follow up? If so, plan how you will do that, as well as praying for that person.

- ❯ Thank God for those who came this session, and pray that he will open their hearts to the truth about Jesus.

- ❯ Pray that the Holy Spirit will open blind eyes to see why Jesus died, and why his death matters to them.

- ❯ Was anyone missing who came last time? Plan to contact them during the week to ask how they are and encourage them to come next time.

Resurrection

▶ *Welcome the group and thank them for coming.*

▶ *Recap on the previous session:*
Last time we saw why Jesus died. He gave his life as a ransom for many. He was punished in our place so that we can be rescued. His death makes it possible for us to be accepted by God and enjoy a relationship with him. We also saw some of the different ways people reacted to Jesus' death.

This time we are going to think about the resurrection of Jesus – did he really rise from the dead and why does it matter?

GROUP ACTIVITY
▶ *If it is appropriate for your group, start the session with one of the activities below. You may also want to look at the activities suggested for the younger age group – STACK ATTACK and EYEWITNESS on pages 79-80 – they may be appropriate for your group.*

HOW HIGH CAN YOU GO?
Aim: This activity is intended to help participants see how important Jesus' resurrection is: without it, Christianity would fall apart.

Equipment: None

- Divide into small groups of 4 or 5.

- Explain that each group has to build a human tower with exactly two feet and four hands touching the ground. The group which lifts one person highest above the ground is the winner.

- Give the groups a few minutes to discuss what they will do; then one minute to build their tower.

- After choosing the winner, ask all the groups to try and remove one hand or foot at a time until they can't move or they collapse.

- **Note:** Do be careful about safety in this game. Do move objects out of the way in case a group falls over. Don't let them try to support the whole group on one wrist!

At the end of the activity, say to participants: "All it takes is for one crucial piece to be removed, and the whole structure collapses. The reason we're talking about the resurrection of Jesus this week is because it is 'the crucial piece' in Christianity."

SCREEN TEST

Aim: To introduce the idea of eyewitnesses.

Equipment: Film clips and equipment to show them on; paper and pens.

- ❯ This game can be played individually or in groups.

- ❯ Show a short (2 minutes or less) film clip – telling the group there will be a quiz about it afterwards.

- ❯ Ask 5-10 difficult observation questions (eg: what colour was the notebook on the desk, which character was wearing glasses, how many trees were in the garden, etc).

- ❯ Read out the correct answers and see who scored the highest.

- ❯ Show a different short film clip. This time ask 5-10 easy observation questions (eg: what was the main character called, did they travel by car or train, how many humps did the camel have, etc).

- ❯ Give the correct answers (if needed!).

At the end of the activity, say to participants: "Some of us are better eyewitnesses than others when looking for tiny details – but it was easy to remember the big, obvious stuff. Today we're going to be thinking about the death and resurrection of Jesus. A dead man coming back to life is something people would be sure to notice! We will see that there were many eyewitnesses who saw that Jesus really did die and rise again."

EXPLORE

▶ *Hand a CY handbook to each participant. Ask them to turn to page 20 and to write down their answer to this question:*

> **What would be your first reaction if you heard that someone had come back from the dead?**

- ❯ Ask the group to share their answers.

- ❯ Most will respond that it is impossible, or certainly not believable: dead people do not come back to life again.

- ❯ A follow-up question could be to ask: "What would you need to know in order to be convinced that someone had actually risen from the dead?" If people say, "I'd need to see it myself", you might respond, "What if someone you trust had seen it, like a close friend or an eyewitness in a court case?"

Note: *It's actually reasonable to be sceptical about someone coming back from the dead – because no one else has. The fact that Jesus came back from the dead highlights his unique identity – after all, no one else is the Son of God! If your group mention Jairus' daughter, who they read about in Session 2, explain that she was brought back to life for a while, but eventually died again. (The same is true for Lazarus.) Only Jesus has beaten death – the first full and true resurrection.*

▶ *Ask everyone to turn to* **Mark 15:42 – 16:8**. *(See note on page 144 about verses 9-20.)*

▶ *Tell the group to listen carefully for four things that surprise the women when they arrive at Jesus' tomb.*

▶ *Ask someone to read the passage aloud and then work through the questions below with the group.*

Why are the women worried as they approach the tomb? (See Mark 16:3.)

● They do not know how they will move the stone.

● It might be helpful to ask what the women were expecting to find. Then point out that none of Jesus' followers were expecting the resurrection. Jesus had told them, but they hadn't understood what he meant (Mark 9:31-32).

Find four things that surprise them when they arrive. (See verses 4-6.)

1. The stone is rolled away.

2. Jesus is not there.

3. A man in white greets them inside the tomb.

4. He tells them that Jesus is risen.

Should they have been surprised that Jesus rose from the dead? (Look at Mark 8:31, 9:30-31, 10:32-34 for clues.)

● In all of these passages, Jesus predicts that his resurrection will happen three days after he has been killed.

● The women should not have been surprised by Jesus' resurrection. In fact, they should have expected it.

Follow-up question: Why were the women and the disciples so surprised at both his death and his resurrection when they had been told repeatedly that it would happen?

● Neither event fitted their expectations. Messiahs don't die. Dead men don't rise!

Why do you think the women ran away from the tomb?

● They were amazed that Jesus had risen from the dead, but they were also afraid because they did not expect it.

● They came looking for "Jesus the Nazarene" – a man from Nazareth – rather than "Jesus Christ, the Son of God".

● They had seen an angel. We know that angels are frightening because they nearly always begin their message by telling people not to be afraid! Eg: Mark 16:6.

● You might ask: What would you have thought had happened to Jesus if you came to the empty tomb?

DVD PRESENTATION

▶ *Watch Episode 5 of the Soul DVD, or deliver Talk 5 using the notes on page 82. The notes for this talk can also be downloaded from www.christianityexplored.org/cy to enable you to adapt them for your group and add your own illustrations.*

▶ *There is a recap (called DOWNLOAD) in the group member's CY Handbook for their reference. Encourage people to write notes on the Download page as they watch the DVD or listen to the talk. The recap is also printed below.*

DOWNLOAD

- If Jesus has not risen from the dead, Christianity collapses.

- The resurrection proves that Jesus is who he says he is, and that his death was a ransom for many.

- Jesus did die: Pontius Pilate, the Roman centurion, Joseph of Arimathea and the women were all certain that Jesus had died.

- Jesus did rise: the tomb was empty; Jesus was seen alive by hundreds of people, many of whom were later killed for insisting that he was alive.

- The resurrection proves that Jesus will come again as Judge of the whole world (Acts 17:31).

- The resurrection means that death has been defeated. If we trust in Jesus, we can have confidence that God will raise us from death.

TALKBACK

▶ *Use the questions below to encourage discussion (they are also printed in the participant's CY Nano Handbook).*

What part of the evidence for Jesus' resurrection do you find most convincing? Why?

- This is to stimulate a general discussion on the evidence.

- Encourage the group to think through the alternatives, eg: "Couldn't Jesus have just fainted?" Answer: No – he'd been through torture, crucifixion and had been stabbed with a spear. The Romans were experts at this – killing was their business. Even if he had simply fainted, could he have rolled back the large stone, avoided a Roman guard and appeared fit and well to his followers soon after? The Roman guard would have been very careful not to let anyone in or out of the tomb, because they knew they might be killed as punishment for failing to do their job properly.

Do you think that Jesus rose from the dead? Why or why not?

- Let people volunteer their answers.

- But if anyone says "no", it's worth gently probing why they don't believe it. Is it that the evidence is not good enough – or is it because they are worried about the implications for them if it is true?

- This may also be the point to introduce the evidence of the changed lives of the first disciples. What turned a frightened group of nobodies into a bold and courageous group of men and women who were prepared to suffer and die for the belief that Jesus had risen from the dead? Would a group of people that preached love and truth-telling base their lives on something they knew to be a lie?

Why does Jesus' resurrection matter, if at all?

- ❯ It matters because, if the resurrection happened as Jesus said it would, then we can trust Jesus on every other point. Jesus is who he says he is. Jesus *did* achieve what he said he would on the cross.

- ❯ Questions about life after death are no longer a matter of opinion – Jesus is able to answer the question, because he has been there and come back.

- ❯ Jesus' resurrection shows that God has accepted Jesus' death as a ransom for many.

- ❯ It also shows that Jesus rules over everyone and everything – even death – and proves that he will return to judge the whole world (Acts 17:31).

Note: *You could unpack this question a bit more by asking: Why, if you trust in Jesus, is the resurrection reassuring? Why, if you don't trust in Jesus, is the resurrection frightening?*

Optional follow up question: Which of the things that Jesus' resurrection proves do you find most scary? Why?

- ❯ Although the thrust of this session has been to present the evidence for the resurrection, one of the reasons why people will not believe good evidence is that they are fearful or hate the implications of its truth for them. So:

  - ❯ The ransom was paid: means that I am truly sin's captive, and in need of saving.

  - ❯ Jesus is Lord: means that he has the right to say what I do with my life, and make moral judgments about what I do and who I am.

  - ❯ Jesus is the returning Judge: means that I will be judged and am responsible for my actions – something most of us would rather not think about.

- ❯ Do not push this discussion at this stage – more of this will come out in subsequent weeks, but it is good to at least point out the possibility that people may be resistant to the evidence because of what it means for them.

▶ *If you have time, now is the moment to answer another of the questions that were asked in the first week's EXPLORE: "If you could ask God one question, and you knew it would be answered, what would it be?"*

▶ *Be careful that you do not over-run on time. It's always better to leave them wanting more and eager to return next time.*

CONCLUSION

▶ *Remind the group about the Inside Track weekend/day away. Give out invitations.*

Finish by encouraging your group members to come back next time. Tell them: We've seen why the resurrection of Jesus is so important to understanding what Christianity is all about. Next time we're going to explore how the death and resurrection of Jesus makes a difference to our lives.

AFTERWARDS

- ❯ Did any of the group members ask a question or make a comment that you could follow up? If so, plan how you will do that, as well as praying for that person.

- ❯ Thank God for those who came this session, and pray that he will open their hearts to the truth about Jesus.

- ❯ Pray that the group members will be able to attend the Inside Track weekend/day away.

- ❯ Was anyone missing who came last time? Plan to contact them during the week to ask how they are and encourage them to next time.

Note on Mark 16:9-20

Your group may ask you about the note in their Bibles which says that some early manuscripts do not include Mark 16:9-20. If so, explain that Mark almost certainly didn't write these verses. He finished his Gospel on the cliffhanger of verse 8. The extra verses were probably added early on by a well-meaning scribe who was making a copy of Mark's Gospel. However, it's worth pointing out that all of the information included in verses 9-20 can also be found elsewhere – either in the other Gospels or Acts – so it's not new or invented material, just a summary of what the rest of the Bible says about the evidence for Jesus' resurrection.

If your group don't ask about these verses, then avoid unnecessary confusion by not mentioning them!

Grace

▶ *Welcome the group and thank them for coming.*

▶ *Recap on the previous session:*
Last time we looked at the evidence for the resurrection and saw that Jesus really did die and then rise to life. We also saw why his resurrection matters: that it proves that death has been beaten, that Jesus will come back to judge everyone, and that God has accepted the ransom that Jesus paid.

This time we are going to see how this makes a difference to our lives.

GROUP ACTIVITY

▶ *If it is appropriate for your group, start the session with one of the activities below. You may also want to look at the activities suggested for the younger age group – SPAGHETTI TOWERS and QUIZ on pages 89-90 – they may be appropriate for your group.*

DOMINO TOWERS

Aim: To illustrate that something that seems impossible can be possible if you know how.

Equipment: Dominos.

- ❯ The aim is to balance 13 dominos on top of a single upright domino. Get people to work in groups to try and do this – they will fail!

- ❯ Demonstrate: place 2 dominoes vertically on the table just a little way apart. Put another domino horizontally resting on these two. Put further 12 dominoes on top, as per pictures: Remove the supporting domino carefully – done right they should balance (**note:** you will need to practice this carefully).

Leader's checklist

Have you...

- ☐ Reminded the group about the next meeting?

- ☐ Collected any items needed for the activities?

- ☐ Enough Bibles or Mark's Gospels for the group?

- ☐ CY Handbooks and pens for each group member?

- ☐ Set up the Soul DVD ready to play? (Or prepared the optional talk and added any personal illustrations.)

- ☐ Thought through your answers to the questions?

- ☐ Travel details for the "Inside Track" weekend/day away?

- ☐ Prayed for each group member and yourself as the leader?

Note: this is an example of a "proposition bet" – a challenge that seems impossible. You can find many more of these on YouTube, by entering the search term "proposition bet". Pick one that is suitable for the group, and your skills!

At the end of the activity, say to your group members: "Some things are impossible for us, because we are thinking about it in the wrong way. In this session, we will discover that the way most people think they can get to know God is wrong."

TIGHT SQUEEZE
Aim: To illustrate that something that seems impossible can be possible if you know how.

Equipment: Sheets of paper (A4 or US Letter size)

- Give each group member a sheet of paper, and tell them there is a prize for anyone who can create a hole and squeeze their whole body through without the paper tearing into 2 pieces.

- This should be impossible for them to do.

- Explain that, although this seems impossible, there is a way. Demonstrate this by folding a sheet of paper and making the cuts indicated by the dotted lines. This should create an intact ring, which you can pass your body through.

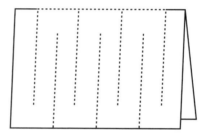

At the end of the activity, say to your group members: "Our sin makes it impossible for us to gain eternal life by our own efforts. But, what is impossible for us is possible for God. In this session we will find out how God makes it possible for us to gain eternal life."

EXPLORE
▶ *Hand a CY Handbook to each participant. Ask them to turn to page 24 and to write down their answer to this question:*

> **What things do people do so others will accept them?**

- This question is intended to get the group thinking about acceptance.

- In general, our sinful world tends to accept people because they have achieved something or because they act or dress in a certain way. It is *conditional* acceptance. We are accepted because of something that we do, or say. When we stop doing that thing, we stop being accepted.

Note: *Don't let this discussion get too long or deep. The aim is simply to start with a few concrete examples from their own experience before moving on to consider the issue of* *being accepted by God. But do be aware of anyone who may be finding the subject of acceptance difficult – this might be something to follow up with them at another time.*

What things do people do to be accepted by God?

❯ This question should reveal something about how people think they should approach and be accepted by God.

❯ Typical answers might include: going to church; being baptized; doing the right things; having Christian parents; being honest and sincere; not harming anyone.

▶ *Ask everyone to turn to **Mark 10:17-22**.*

▶ *Ask someone to read the passage aloud and then work through the questions below with the group. Although these questions are the same this time as the ones for the younger age-group in CY Nano – older teens and young adults will naturally answer them in greater depth.*

Why does the man think God should accept him?

❯ He claims that he has kept the commandments since he was a boy (verse 20). He thinks that God should accept him because he has kept this set of rules.

What is Jesus' response?

❯ Jesus tells him that he should go and sell all he has and give money to the poor. And then follow him.

Why does the man leave? What does that show about the man?

❯ The man leaves because he does not want to do what Jesus has asked him. He has a lot of money and chooses this above following Jesus.

❯ Jesus has shown the man that he has broken the very first commandment (see Exodus 20:2–3). He had made money into a god – it was more important to him than his Creator.

❯ Like the man, people sometimes think God will accept them because of good things they've done. But like the man, however good we think we are, we all put "things" in place of God (eg: popularity, image, comfort, good grades, money etc).

Note: *Jesus is not teaching that Christians should have no money. He is teaching that money should not take the place of God – and if something does, we should remove it from our lives. Jesus isn't teaching that giving money would earn God's favour either – rather, he is showing that money was the thing keeping the man from following Jesus.*

If God asked you: "Why should I give you eternal life?", what would you say?

- If you are using the Soul DVD, you will need to ask the group to think about this question beforehand. If you are using the talk notes from CY Nano, this question is built into the talk.

DVD PRESENTATION

▶ *Watch Episode 6 of the Soul DVD, or deliver Talk 6 using the notes on page 92. The notes for this talk can also be downloaded from www.christianityexplored.org/cy to enable you to adapt them for your group and add your own illustrations.*

▶ *There is a recap (called DOWNLOAD) in the group member's CY Handbook for their reference. Encourage people to write notes on the Download page as they watch the DVD or listen to the talk. The recap is also printed below.*

DOWNLOAD

- Most people think God will accept them because of things they have done or haven't done. But these things can't solve the problem of sin.

- The Bible tells us that God accepts us, not because of anything *we've* done, but because of what *Jesus* has done.

- Like the man with the skin disease, we need to ask Jesus to make us clean (Mark 1:40-42).

- The only way we can be accepted by God is because he sent Jesus to die on the cross in our place.

- Grace is God's undeserved gift to us. Because of what Jesus has done, God treats us in a way we don't deserve.

TALKBACK

▶ *Use the questions below to encourage discussion (they are also printed in the participant's CY Handbook).*

What exactly is grace? How would you explain it if someone asked you?

- Grace is God's undeserved gift to us.

- We deserve to be punished for our sin, but grace is God forgiving us when we don't deserve it.

What do people find offensive about grace? What does it say about us?

- It tells us that we are hopeless and helpless without it.

- Many people hate this idea – we tend to be proud of ourselves and of our own achievements.

Note: *you might like to look up and read Ephesians 2:8-9 at this point to reinforce this point.*

What is so wonderful about grace? What does it offer us?

❯ The free gift of eternal life.

❯ It offers us new life, freedom to follow God, a fresh start with Jesus in control, etc.

❯ It means we can be real with God and not try to hide our mistakes when we mess up.

What does grace tell us about the character of God?

❯ He is amazing! He is prepared to forgive me, welcome me into his family, and he himself has paid the price of my wrongdoing through the death of Jesus on the cross.

CONCLUSION

▶ *Remind the group about the Inside Track weekend/day away – and confirm any travel arrangements.*

Finish by encouraging your group members to come to the Inside Track weekend/day away, and also to come back next time. Tell them: We've seen that forgiveness is a gift, paid for by Jesus Christ. Next time we're going to find out how we can receive that gift. We'll discover what it means to be a Christian.

AFTERWARDS

❯ Did any of the group members ask a question or make a comment that you could follow up? If so, plan how you will do that, as well as praying for that person.

❯ Thank God for those who came this session, and pray that he will open their hearts to the truth about Jesus.

❯ Pray that the Holy Spirit will convict group members of their need to accept the gift of forgiveness. If any are already Christians, pray that they will grow in their understanding of God's grace and have the courage to talk openly about their faith in Jesus.

❯ Pray that the group members will be able to attend the *Inside Track* weekend/day away. Plan to follow up any who haven't let you know whether they are coming.

Inside Track

The *Inside Track* weekend/day away is an important part of the *CY* course as it will give your group members an opportunity to count the cost of being a Christian and consider the implications for their own lives. The *Inside Track* material is designed to be used in between Sessions 6 and 7 of the course.

The weekend/day away will give more time to find out about what it's like being a Christian, and the gifts God gives us to help us live for him. The following four themes will be covered:

- Introduction: It's tough to follow Jesus

- Session 1: Holy Spirit

- Session 2: Church

- Session 3: Talk *(the Bible and prayer)*

Being away together allows more time for reflection and for personal testimonies as your group gets an "inside track" on what it's like being a Christian. It will also give them time to observe how you and your co-leaders live out your own faith in Jesus. They will get part of their "inside track" by looking at you!

You will find all the material for the *Inside Track* weekend/day away in Section 4 of this Leader's manual, starting on page 161.

So what?

▶ *Welcome the group and thank them for coming.*

▶ *Recap on the previous session:*
Last time we saw that God accepts us not because of anything *we've* done, but because of what *Jesus* has done. Like the man with the skin disease, we need to ask Jesus to make us clean. We thought about grace – God's undeserved gift to us – and we saw that forgiveness is a gift, paid for by Jesus.

If you did the Inside Track programme after week 6, also include this summary: And we saw on our weekend/day away that the Christian life is brilliant, but tough.

This time we are going to find out exactly what it means to be a Christian.

GROUP ACTIVITY

▶ *If it is appropriate for your group, start the session with one of the activities below. You may also want to look at the activities suggested for the younger age group – TANGRAMS and FOLLOW THE LEADER on pages 101-102 – they may be appropriate for your group.*

WHAT IS IT?
Aim: To show that you need to put all the pieces together to make a complete picture.

Equipment: Digital camera, data projector, computer.

- ❯ Take some pictures of ordinary objects using a digital camera.

- ❯ You could include things around the room you use for CY, and even the faces of people in the group.

- ❯ Show the images in close up, and slowly zoom out until someone guesses what it is.

- ❯ Award a prize for the winner.

At the end of the activity, say to your group: "Sometimes it's only when you see all the pieces together that you can understand the whole thing. It's a bit like that with Christianity sometimes. It's easy to misunderstand

Leader's checklist

Have you...

- ☐ Collected any items needed for the activities?

- ☐ Enough Bibles or Mark's Gospels for the group?

- ☐ CY Handbooks and pens for each group member?

- ☐ Set up the Soul DVD ready to play? (Or prepared the optional talk and added any personal illustrations.)

- ☐ Thought through your answers to the questions?

- ☐ Details of things the group members might choose to do next?

- ☐ Prayed for each group member and yourself as the leader?

unless you've got hold of the big picture. Today we're going to put all the pieces together to see the whole picture of who Jesus is, why he came, and what it means to follow him."

COPYCAT

Aim: To show that following Jesus will be difficult.

Equipment: Pens and paper, flipchart.

- ❯ Form teams and give a picture of an object (a chair, a train, a cooling fan, etc.) to one person from each team. Tell them that they have 10 seconds to draw it, and then they must hand their copy on to the next member of their team. None of the rest of the team may see the original.

- ❯ The copy gets passed on to the next person, who has to draw what they see. This new copy is then passed on again. This continues until the final version is handed to the last person in the team, who must then guess what it is.

- ❯ This game can be done any number of ways. For example, you could use modelling clay, where the next person gets to see the model, and must then squash the clay flat and recreate it before handing on to the next. Alternatively, do it as a serial game of charades, where you give an activity to act out silently to the first person in the team (eg: serving dinner on an aircraft, changing a car wheel, etc.) who acts it to the second person, who acts it to the third, etc. The last person has to guess what it is.

At the end of the activity, say to your group: "Today we're going to be thinking about what is involved in following Jesus. In the game we played, the instructions got more and more unclear, but we are going to hear very clearly from Jesus himself about what it means to follow him."

EXPLORE

❯ *Hand a CY Handbook to each participant. Ask them to turn to page 34 and to write down their answer to this question:*

> **We started CY by asking: "If you could ask God one question, what would it be?" If God were to ask *you* one question, what do you think it would it be?**

- ❯ This question will reveal how much your group has absorbed over the last seven weeks. You might get things like:

  - ❯ What is stopping you from believing in me?

  - ❯ Why haven't you put your trust in Jesus?

  - ❯ Why don't you tell others about me?

  - ❯ What are you doing with your life / your gifts?

- ❯ If you get a silly answer, welcome their comment, but try and draw people back to the serious question. It might help to rephrase the question as: "If God were to ask you one question about your faith or relationship with him, what would it be?"

- ❯ As this is the final session you should follow up by asking your group: "How might you answer God if he asked you that?"

▶ *Ask everyone to turn to* **Mark 1:14-15**.

▶ *Ask someone to read the passage aloud and then work through the questions below with the group.*

What do you think Jesus means by "the good news of God"?

- ❷ This question helps to reveal if your group has understood what the gospel is.

- ❷ It is the good news that Jesus, God's Son, came into this world, lived a perfect life, died for us on the cross, rose from the dead and is in heaven today. It is the good news that whoever repents and believes in him will be "ransomed from judgment", accepted by God and enjoy a relationship with him forever.

Follow-up question: We talked in session 1 about some of the ways that Christianity appears to be bad news: boring, irrelevant, untrue. As the weeks have gone by, have you changed your view on this?

- ❷ Their answers will hopefully show that group members have grown in their understanding and/or changed their thinking – which should be encouraging!

What does Jesus mean when he says: "The time has come" and "The kingdom of God is near"?

- ❷ It is like saying: "This is it" – the time that everyone has been waiting for is here.

- ❷ God's kingdom – his power and authority over everything – is being shown in Jesus' life, death and resurrection.

What do you think the word "repent" means?

- ❷ We haven't discussed repentance yet in the course, but your group members may have some ideas about what it means. If they think it just means "saying sorry", help them to understand its fuller meaning by explaining the following points:

    - ❷ Repentance is a complete inner change of our attitude towards God and other people.

    - ❷ It begins with a sincere apology to God for our sin because we realize that it has offended him. We then turn from living our own way and start to live God's way.

    - ❷ That means being *for* what Jesus is *for*, and *against* what he is *against*.

- ❷ You could illustrate repentance as completely turning around *from* having your back to God, *to* facing him and walking towards him; living a life that has him as the destination of all that we do. You can act out turning around, which helps communicate the point.

What do you think it means to "believe the good news"?

- ❷ To believe means more than just saying something is true. It means:

1. We know about Jesus and what he has done.

2. We are convinced that these things about Jesus are true.

3. We place our trust in Jesus and obey him.

4. We relate to him as who he really is – the Lord – by doing as he does, thinking as he thinks.

❷ Believing is more than "knowing" the truth – it means "living" the truth.

DVD PRESENTATION

▶ *Watch Episode 7 of the Soul DVD, or deliver Talk 7 using the notes on page 104. The notes for this talk can also be downloaded from www.christianityexplored.org/cy to enable you to adapt them for your group and add your own illustrations.*

▶ *There is a recap (called DOWNLOAD) in the group member's CY Handbook for their reference. Encourage people to write notes on the Download page as they watch the DVD or listen to the talk. The recap is also printed below.*

DOWNLOAD

❷ A Christian is someone who knows who Jesus is: the Son of God, the "Christ", the King who was promised throughout the Old Testament.

❷ A Christian is someone who understands why Jesus came: he came to die as the only way sinful people can be brought back into a relationship with God.

❷ A Christian is someone who follows Jesus: Jesus says: "If anyone would come after me, he must deny himself and take up his cross and follow me" (Mark 8:34). Denying self means no longer living for ourselves but for Jesus and others. Taking up our cross means being prepared to follow him, whatever the cost.

❷ Jesus gives a convincing reason to live like this: "Whoever loses his life for me and for the gospel will save it" (Mark 8:35). If we give our lives to him, he will save them. We will know and enjoy God now, and spend eternity with him when we die.

TALKBACK

▶ *Use the questions below to encourage discussion (they are also printed in the participant's CY Handbook).*

How would you score the following statements? (0 = completely unconvinced; 10 = very sure)

Jesus is God.

Jesus came to rescue us from our sin.

Following Jesus means denying ourselves and putting Jesus first, whatever the cost.

---

❷ These questions are designed to see how much the group has absorbed about the content of the Christian message during the CY course.

Follow-up question: There's a lot at stake in your answers to these questions. If the gospel is true, then you must believe it – whatever the cost. Have the implications of the gospel for your life made it harder for you to accept the truth of the facts about Jesus, even though there is very good evidence?

What choices will you make now that you've finished CY? What is the next step for you?

- Write down everyone's answer so you can plan a way ahead and pray for them appropriately.

- You need gently to encourage people to opt for one of three routes:

  1. "I need more time to think." Even if someone thinks that Jesus is definitely not for them, encourage them not to close the door but to keep putting themselves in the place where they will hear about Jesus and spend time with those who follow him. For others who genuinely do not have enough information or need more time to absorb and think through the gospel message, the same encouragement is appropriate.

  2. "I would like to become a Christian." It would be good for anyone who has reached this point to see if they really understand what repentance means.

  3. "I know I'm a Christian. I want to live for Jesus in every part of my life, whatever the cost." Any of your group members who are already Christians can be challenged to count the cost of living for Jesus every day. There may be particular areas of their life where they need to repent and to ask the Holy Spirit to help them live wholeheartedly for Jesus.

- It may be appropriate to say a prayer of commitment with the whole group – see below and the note on the next page. There is also an alternative prayer which may be more appropriate if some or all of your group are not ready to follow Christ.

CONCLUSION

▶ *As this is the end of the course, expand upon the choices now available to group members. This could include handing out church details or invites to a youth group. Don't forget to follow up with each of the group members (see "After the Course" in Section 1 of this book).*

▶ *Make sure you have answered all of the questions from session 1.*

You could close by saying: Thank you for coming to CY. I really hope you've enjoyed it. If you've become convinced of who Jesus is and what he came to do, and you understand what it will mean to follow him, you may want to echo the following prayer quietly in your own heart:

Heavenly Father, I have rebelled against you. I have sinned in my thoughts, my words and my actions. I am sorry for the way I have lived and ask you to forgive me. Thank you so much that Jesus died on the cross so that I could be forgiven. Thank you that Jesus rose again and is ruling as King over everyone and everything. Please send your Holy Spirit so that I can follow Jesus whatever the cost and live with him as King of my life. Amen.

If you did pray that prayer, let me know – I'd love to help you start living as a Christian.

Note: *Depending on your group, you may find the following prayer helpful instead of or as well as the one above:*

> **Dear God, there are so many questions in my mind, and so many things I am unsure of. Thank you for the time we have spent looking at Mark's Gospel and for the people in this group. Thank you that we now know more about who Jesus is and why he came. Please help me to find answers to my questions, as I learn more about Jesus. And help us to understand the greatness of your love for each one of us in sending your Son Jesus to die for us. Amen.**

▶ *Explain to the group that you want to know what they thought of CY, so that you can do it better next time. Ask them to fill out the FEEDBACK FORM (hand them out). Assure them that their forms will be treated with strict confidence, and not shown to anyone else.*

Note: Prayers of commitment

We've included these two prayers as ways you might want to try to encourage some kind of response to what group members have been hearing about during CY. But you need to be clear about what a prayer does and doesn't do:

- ❯ **It is a helpful way of wrapping up.** People, especially young people, often appreciate the concreteness of a prayer of commitment. It is a helpful way of bringing together the many feelings and thoughts they will have had during the course.

- ❯ **It doesn't make them a Christian.** Only genuine, deep-down, Spirit-worked faith and repentance will turn someone from a sinner on their way to hell into a "saint" who is bound for glory.

- ❯ **So use with caution.** If someone prays a prayer and says they mean it, you should start to treat them as a believer, and encourage them to think of themselves as a believer. But you should also look for, and pray for, evidence that God is genuinely at work in them. Do they have a growing consciousness of sin and are starting to hate it? Do they love meeting with other believers? Do they want to pray? Do they hunger to read the Bible and to hear good teaching?

We have suggested that you offer one of the two prayers we have included, depending on the kind of people in the group, and whether you think it is right. But you may want to handle it differently, and encourage individuals to approach you if they really want to become a Christian. In this setting, they can be encouraged to pray a prayer like this. Alternatively, you could offer to give each group member a copy of an appropriate evangelistic booklet which includes a prayer of commitment, and encourage them to read, think and then pray this prayer if they want to.

AFTERWARDS

❯ Did any of the group members say they would like to find out more or attend another course? If so, plan how you will follow that up, as well as praying for that person.

❯ Thank God for all those who came on the course, and for giving you the privilege of sharing the good news about Jesus with them.

❯ Pray for those who have said they need more time to think. Pray that the Holy Spirit will convict them of their need to accept the gift of forgiveness.

❯ If any are already Christians, pray that they will grow in their understanding of God's grace and have the courage to talk openly about their faith in Jesus.

Name

1 Before you began CY, how would you have described yourself?

☐ I didn't believe in God

☐ I wasn't sure if God existed or not

☐ I believed in God but not in Jesus Christ

☐ A Christian

☐ Something else

2 Now that you've finished CY, how would you describe yourself?

☐ I understand who Jesus is, why he came and what it means to follow him. I have put my trust in him.

☐ I wouldn't call myself a Christian, but I would like to find out more.

☐ Other

3 If you have not yet put your trust in Jesus, what is stopping you?

4 What would you like to do now?

☐ I am interested in joining a follow-up course (a course that will help me to continue in the Christian life).

☐ I'd like to read the Christianity Explored book to help me remember what I discovered.

☐ I don't want to do anything more at this stage.

☐ I would like to join a church.

☐ I am happy at the church I go to.

5 On a scale of 1 to 10 how much did you enjoy CY?
(1 = I really hated it; 10 = I really loved it.)

6 Anything else you'd like to tell us?

Inside Track
Weekend/Day Away

Before you go

Jesus urged people to count the cost of following him before making a decision to do so. In the same way, your group needs to have a clear understanding of what the Christian life involves before committing to it. With this in mind, the *Inside Track* weekend or day away has been placed before Session 7 – the final session – when group members are invited to repent and believe.

The material covered during this time aims to paint a realistic picture of what the Christian life is like, and to reassure people that they will not be alone if they choose to begin following Christ. Participants are helped to see that being a Christian is both wonderful and tough – and are assured that God will graciously provide his Holy Spirit, the church family, the Bible and prayer to help them.

▶ *In Session 3, you should let the group know that there will be a weekend or day away. Give a brief idea of what will happen, and let them know that, if they are under 18, they will need their parents' permission to attend.*

▶ *In Sessions 4 and 5, remind the group about the weekend or day away. Have spare invitations available for anyone who missed a previous session or has lost their invite. Encourage group members to let you know if they're coming, and to return their parents' permission slip (if needed).*

▶ *In Session 6 hand out schedules for the weekend or day away, and confirm any travel arrangements for getting to the venue.*

▶ *Ensure that your prayer team has been notified and that they are praying ahead.*

Note: On the whole in CY we have tried to teach from chunks of the Bible rather than single verses, and, given that it has all been from Mark, the context is generally pretty clear. However, the *Inside Track* material refers to other parts of the Bible as well as Mark. We have tried to do this carefully so as to avoid taking any verses out of context. But you may decide that it's worth making some talks a sentence or two longer if necessary to ensure that the young people realise we are genuinely teaching what the Bible is saying and not taking it out of context to suit our own ends.

Planning the programme
The weekend or day away allows plenty of time for leaders to continue to build trusting relationships with group members. Use the free time for activities that will facilitate this (for example, playing a team sport or making something together).

Testimonies from members of the youth group and/or leaders are also important, because they give participants an insight into the practicalities of Christian living. Choose some people to present their testimonies and help them to prepare what they will say. Testimonies can be presented at any point during the weekend or day away.

Make sure that the people you ask to talk about their faith in Christ are prepared to talk not just about an exciting or dramatic conversion experience. The aim of *Inside Track* is to help people to have a deeper insight into the experience of being a believer. Those who speak or lead should share both the difficulties and cost of being a follower of Jesus, but also the sense of peace and assurance that we are forgiven and accepted by our heavenly Father, the joy of knowing Christ, and the comfort and encouragement that the Holy Spirit gives us.

Think carefully beforehand about whether to include singing or praying in your programme. These are both natural parts of a Christian life – so you could see them as being part of giving people an "inside track" on what it's like to be a Christian. But you need to be careful not to do anything that could make participants feel unduly pressured or uncomfortable. If you do decide to sing, be aware that many songs are written from the point of view of a believer, using phrases such as "I love you Lord", "I will praise you", "You are my God". You don't want to be putting words into a participant's mouth, or assuming a belief they may not have – so try instead to choose songs that teach truth *about* God the Father, and about Jesus.

In a similar way, don't expect people to join in with a prayer that implies belief, or a commitment to live for God. However, prayer is a wonderful way to model the relationship a Christian has with their loving Father – as you thank him for his goodness and ask him to help you know him better through his word, the Bible. It might help to explain that "Amen" means "we agree", and is therefore a way for others to join in with a prayer and make it their own. Do assure group members that it's fine just to listen quietly during a prayer, and not to feel they have to join in.

Inside Track Checklist

There will be plenty of practical things to arrange for the *Inside Track* weekend/day away. Use the following list as a starting point.

- ☐ If your group includes under 18s, follow the child protection policy for your church or organisation.

- ☐ Book the venue and make sure everyone knows how to get there.

- ☐ Give group members a list of what to bring (and what not to bring!). Let them know about anything they might need money for (eg: special activities, book stall). Check if they need to take bedding if you're going away for a weekend.

- ☐ Arrange catering for the time away, including any special dietary requirements.

- ☐ Ask group members for any health or allergy information. You will also need parental permission to give medical assistance for anyone who is under 18.

- ☐ Ask for parental permission to take any under 18s away with the group, and for phone numbers in case you need to contact parents while you're away.

- ☐ Check whether you are covered by the insurance for your church or organisation. If not, arrange separate insurance cover.

- ☐ Plan the programme, including any organised activities.

- ☐ If you are able to attend a local church on the Sunday, let them know you are coming.

- ☐ Produce a programme for the weekend /day. Give copies to your group members, and also to anyone who will be praying for you.

- ☐ If you will be away from your usual venue, check what the facilities will be for projecting powerpoint slides or other audio-visual needs. Arrange for spare Bibles to be available for anyone who has forgotten theirs.

- ☐ Ask Christian group members and/or leaders to give short testimonies. Arrange to meet with them beforehand to help them prepare. Make sure that they will be realistic about the cost of discipleship, as well as the assurance, comfort and encouragement that they have received from God.

- ☐ Plan the talks, Bible studies, answers to questions, etc before you go – there won't be time while you're there!

EXAMPLE SCHEDULE FOR A WEEKEND AWAY

ACTIVITY	TIME
FRIDAY	
Arrive	7:00 p.m.
Welcome followed by organized activities	7:30 p.m.
SATURDAY	
Leaders' prayer meeting	8:30 a.m.
Breakfast	9:00 a.m.
Introduction – CY It's Tough to Follow Jesus	10:00 a.m.
Session 1 – Holy Spirit/CY You Need the Holy Spirit followed by TALKBACK	10:30 a.m.
Lunch	12:00 p.m.
Free afternoon / Organized activities	1:00 p.m.
Dinner	6:00 p.m.
Session 2 – Church/CY The Church is Your Family followed by TALKBACK	7:00 p.m.
Free evening / Organized activities	8:30 p.m.
SUNDAY	
Leaders' prayer meeting	8:30 a.m.
Breakfast	9:00 a.m.
Attend church with your group if possible	10:00 a.m.
Lunch	12:00 p.m.
Session 3 – Talk/CY It's Good to Talk followed by TALKBACK	1:00 p.m.
Conclusion	2:15 p.m.
Leave	2:30 p.m.

EXAMPLE SCHEDULE FOR A DAY AWAY

ACTIVITY	TIME
Arrive	10:00 a.m.
Welcome	10:30 a.m.
Introduction – CY It's Tough to Follow Jesus	10:45 a.m.
Session 1 – Holy Spirit/CY You Need the Holy Spirit followed by TALKBACK	11:00 a.m.
Lunch	12:30 p.m.
Free afternoon / Organized activities	1:30 p.m.
Session 2 – Church/CY The Church is Your Family followed by TALKBACK	3:30 p.m.
Break	5:00 p.m.
Session 3 – Talk/CY It's Good to Talk followed by TALKBACK	5:30 p.m.
Conclusion	6:45 p.m.
Leave	7:00 p.m.

Inside Track

Note: There are sample programmes for the *Inside Track* weekend/day away on pages 166-167 of this Leader's Guide. This material is an important part of the CY or CY Nano course as it will give your group members an opportunity to count the cost of being a Christian and consider the implications for their own lives. Being away together allows more time for reflection and for personal testimonies as your group gets an "inside track" on what it's like being a Christian. It will also give them time to observe how you and your co-leaders live out your own faith in Jesus. They will get part of their "inside track" by looking at you!

Although the *Inside Track* material is the same for both CY and CY Nano, specific questions and "downloads" are sometimes worded differently in the two handbooks. When this happens, both versions are printed in these leader's notes.

▶ *Welcome the group and thank them for coming to the Inside Track weekend/day away. Go through the programme with them so that they know what to expect. The exact programme will depend on how long you are away for, and whether you are building in extra activities, but it will need to include the following:*

- Introduction: CY it's tough to follow Jesus

- Session 1. The Holy Spirit: CY we need the Holy Spirit

- Session 2. The church: CY the church is your family

- Session 3. The Bible and prayer: CY it's good to talk

- Conclusion

INTRODUCTION

This talk introduces the theme for the weekend/day away. It is very short and can be given just before the opening session on the Holy Spirit. This talk must be delivered "live" – there is no material for the *Inside Track* sessions on the Soul DVD.

▶ *Deliver the Introduction: **CY it's tough to follow Jesus**, using the notes below. The notes for this talk can also be downloaded from www.christianityexplored.org/cy to enable you to adapt them for your group and add your own illustrations.*

OUTLINE OF INTRODUCTORY TALK: CY IT'S TOUGH TO FOLLOW JESUS

▣ *Use the outline below to develop your own talk. This outline can also be downloaded from www.christianityexplored.org/cy*

Aim

➲ To show that it's wonderful being a Christian – but it's also tough.

➲ To see that God gives us help – the Holy Spirit, the church, the Bible and prayer.

Note: *It's often easier for people to hear a negative message ("it's tough") than a positive one ("it's wonderful") – so think of ways in which your talk can emphasize the thrill of being a Christian, eg: the tone of your voice, personal testimony, etc.*

Opening

▣ *In the past six sessions the group has read about a number of people who met Jesus. Choose one of the following activities to remind them of some of these people:*

1. *Play hangman to discover three people who met Jesus. The group have to work out the description by playing hangman in the usual way, and then guess who it describes. Eg: "forgiven and healed by Jesus" (paralysed man), "invited his friends to meet Jesus" (Levi), "went away from Jesus sad" (rich man).*

2. *Stick up twenty pieces of paper around the walls. On ten, write the names of people who met Jesus; on the other ten, describe what happened when they met Jesus. Give group members a blank sheet of paper each. They need to match people with their descriptions and write down the answers. (This is easiest if you label each description from A to J, eg: A: brought back to life by Jesus; B: saw how Jesus died and said he was the Son of God, etc.)*

3. *Ask your group how many people they can remember and what happened to them as a result of meeting Jesus. Depending on your group, you might prefer to ask them to do this in pairs or small groups, and then feed the answers back to you. Between them (maybe with a little prompting from you!) they should come up with the following:*

   ➲ *Paralysed man – Jesus forgave his sins and healed him (Mark 2:1-12)*

   ➲ *Disciples – rescued from drowning when Jesus calmed the storm (Mark 4:35-41)*

   ➲ *Demon-possessed man – his life was transformed when Jesus threw out the demons (Mark 5:1-20)*

   ➲ *Woman who had been bleeding for 12 years – Jesus healed her (Mark 5:25-34)*

   ➲ *Jairus and his daughter – Jesus brought Jairus' daughter back to life (Mark 5:21-24, 35-43)*

   ➲ *Levi the tax collector – left his job to follow Jesus, invited his friends to meet Jesus (Mark 2:13-17)*

   ➲ *Roman centurion – saw how Jesus died and said that he was the Son of God (Mark 15:39)*

- *Pontius Pilate – knew Jesus was innocent but still handed him over to be crucified (Mark 15:15)*

- *Rich man – went away from Jesus sad because he had great wealth (Mark 10:17-22)*

- *Man with skin disease – Jesus healed him (Mark 1:40-45)*

- *Try to keep the focus on the main characters, but you may find they also mention others who were present – the friends who brought the paralysed man, teachers of the law who disapproved, pigs (!), Jairus' family, teacher of the law who asked what the greatest commandment is, soldiers who crucified Jesus, religious leaders who watched Jesus die.*

- Some of the people who met Jesus had their lives completely changed as a result. Some were seriously ill, but Jesus healed them. The disciples were in danger of drowning in a terrible storm, but Jesus stopped the storm and saved them. The man whose life was ruined by evil spirits had his life transformed when Jesus made the demons leave him. Jairus' daughter was even brought back to life. All of these people had their lives changed wonderfully by Jesus.

- But did you notice that following Jesus also has a cost? Levi, the tax collector, left his job to follow Jesus. And the rich man went away sad when Jesus told him to sell everything he had and give the money away.

- Following Jesus means a huge change in our lives. Being a Christian is great. But it's also tough. We need to make changes to how we live – changes that our family and friends will notice, and often won't like. There will be things we need to stop doing, which our friends and family will be puzzled, hurt or offended by. And there will be things that we need to start doing which our friends and family may not like. And we may find that we get laughed at, or worse, by people who are close to us.

▶ *You may want to include a personal testimony here giving an example of how it is both wonderful and tough living as a Christian. You might also want to refer to Mark 3:31-35; Mark 6:1-6 to show that Jesus had exactly the same experience. The testimony could be from you, another leader or a group member who is a Christian. If you ask a group member, do give them plenty of advance notice and plan time for them to discuss what they want to say with you or a co-leader beforehand.*

- It's great following Jesus, but it's also tough, so God gives us four things to help us:

  - The Holy Spirit – this is the Spirit of Jesus, who helps us to live for him.

  - The church – this means other Christians, who will encourage us to keep going.

  - The Bible and prayer – these are gifts from God to help us to grow to know him more and more.

- During this *Inside Track* weekend we'll find out more about these gifts God gives us as we get the "inside track" on what it's really like to be a Christian.

SESSION 1: SPIRIT

GROUP ACTIVITY

▶ *Choose one of the following activities, to suit your group and the time you have available. If your weekend/day away is held somewhere with more space than your usual venue, choose an activity you wouldn't usually be able to do.*

GUIDE THE WAY

Aim: To show that God leads his people by his Spirit.

Equipment: Blindfolds (airline sleep masks work well); baby's "shape sorter" puzzle.

- ❯ Split the group into small teams of around four each.

- ❯ Give each group a blindfold. One person in each group should be blindfolded, and the others in their group are responsible for "directing" that person to do a particular task. Do not tell them what the task is until all the blindfolds have been put on.

- ❯ Tell the teams their task: "You must direct your blindfolded team member to pick up a block and put it in the correctly-shaped hole. You must not touch your team mate in any way, and the first one to complete the task wins."

At the end of the activity, say to your group: "You needed to be guided to pick up a block and put it in the correct hole. It is impossible to live as a Christian without the Holy Spirit to guide you."

LOUD OBSTACLE COURSE RELAY

Aim: To show that God leads his people by his Spirit.

Equipment: Blindfolds; equipment to set up an obstacle course, megaphones (optional).

- ❯ Set up a long obstacle course – outside if possible. There may already be suitable obstacles outside (eg: tree trunks or a small stream) or you could use tables, hoops etc. Be careful not to create a course that's unsafe. Depending on the age of your group members, you may also want warn them that they might get wet or muddy.

- ❯ Divide your group into two teams; then ask each team to divide into pairs. One member of each pair puts on a blindfold, the other will be their "director". If possible put on the blindfolds before the group see the obstacle course – and then ask the "directors" to carefully lead their partners to the start of the course.

- ❯ The blindfolded members line up at one end of the course; the "directors" line up opposite them at the other end. Give the front "director" from each team a megaphone.

- ❯ When you give the signal to start, both "directors" have to shout instructions to their partners to guide them safely down the obstacle course. As soon as their partner safely finished the course, the megaphone is handed on to the next "director", who starts to shout instructions to his/her partner.

- ❯ The team who are first to safely guide all of their blindfolded members through the course are the winners.

At the end of the activity, say to your group: "You needed lots of guidance to safely make it through the obstacles. It is impossible to live as a Christian without the Holy Spirit to guide you."

BLIND GOAL SHOOTING

Aim: To show that God leads his people by his Spirit.

Equipment: Blindfolds; goal posts or markers; a football, or hockey stick and ball, for each team.

- Divide your group into two or more teams. Choose a "director" for each team.

- Set up a set of goal posts or markers for each team (make sure they are the same distance apart for each team!)

- Line the teams up opposite their goals; then place the football (or hockey stick and ball) halfway between the team and the goal.

- The first member of each team is blindfolded; then turned around three times by a leader. The "director" then shouts instructions to guide the team member to the ball and attempt to shoot it into the goal.

- Each member of the team has a turn at being blindfolded, turned around three times, and trying to score a goal. No one other than the "director" is allowed to call out any instructions and no one other than a leader is allowed to turn them around.

- The team that scores the most goals wins.

At the end of the activity, say to your group: "You needed lots of guidance to score a goal. It is impossible to live as a Christian without the Holy Spirit to guide you."

TALK 1: THE HOLY SPIRIT/CY WE NEED THE HOLY SPIRIT

▷ *This talk must be delivered "live" – there is no material for the Inside Track sessions on the Soul DVD. Deliver Talk 1 using the notes below. The notes for this talk can also be downloaded from www.christianityexplored.org/cy to enable you to adapt them for your group and add your own illustrations.*

▷ *There is a recap (called DOWNLOAD) in the participant's CY or CY Nano Handbook for their reference. Encourage people to write notes on the Download page as they listen to the talk.*

OUTLINE OF TALK 1: CY WE NEED THE HOLY SPIRIT

▷ *Use the outline below to develop your own talk. This outline can also be downloaded from www.christianityexplored.org/cy*

Aim

- To explain that being a Christian is to have God living in our lives, changing us from the inside out.

- To show that being a Christian is both wonderful and tough.

- To explain what Jesus means when he calls the Holy Spirit "Counsellor".

- To describe how the Holy Spirit guides us, shows us our sin and gives us the desire to please God.

- To explain that being a Christian is impossible by ourselves – but God gives us his Spirit to help us.

Opening

- We're going to be thinking about what it's like to be a follower of Jesus. The first thing to say is that it is great. Being a Christian is about knowing that your sins are forgiven.

- We saw in the story of the paralysed man (Mark 2:1-10) that his friends (and probably he) thought his greatest need was healing. Jesus knew that forgiveness is our greatest need, because sin is the obstacle that prevents us from having a friendship with our loving Creator.

- It's the same with us. Whatever problems you may have – and many of them are real, and deeply felt – your greatest need is to have your sins forgiven.

▶ *You may want to illustrate this point with things your particular group may relate to as "felt needs": a boyfriend/girlfriend; good grades at school; sense of significance; self-fulfillment; acceptance with others, etc. Try to make your examples very concrete!*

- We saw in Jesus' teaching in Mark 7 that sin comes from deep within us. He said that it's out of the heart that come "evil thoughts, sexual immorality, theft, murder, adultery, greed, malice, deceit, lewdness, envy, slander, arrogance, and folly" (Mark 7:21-22). Something big needs to happen to our sinful hearts if we're going to change.

- That "big thing" is at the centre of what it means to be a Christian. We looked in the last session at what grace means. Being a Christian is not about trying to be a better person in our own strength. The truth is we can't become a better person – because what's at the centre of us – our hearts – are sinful. We can't change our hearts from the outside in.

▶ *You could remind them of the illustration of sin as a disease (used in the talk for session 4). The spots on the skin are the symptoms of disease in your blood. You don't heal the disease by putting band aids (sticking plasters) on the spots – you need medicine to destroy the disease in your blood. Then the spots will go away.*

- The Bible tells us that only God can change us from the inside out. God does an amazing thing. He has promised that he will come and live in our hearts, and change us from the inside out.

- We just saw in the game we played how we find some things impossible without help from someone else. Some of you were guided pretty badly and found it doubly difficult! But, if you're a Christian, you have the perfect helper: God the Holy Spirit.

- We're going to look at what Jesus says about the Holy Spirit in John chapter 14.

Note: *These Inside Track talks will look at several books of the Bible, not just Mark's Gospel, so it will be helpful if you give your group page numbers for the Bible references.*

▶ *Read aloud* **John 14:15-18**.

1. Who is the Holy Spirit?

- Jesus promises that those who trust him will have a "Counsellor" – in other words, a helper, comforter, guide, instructor – who will live with them and in them.

- Jesus says "*another* Counsellor". He is saying that this Counsellor will do for his followers what he himself did for them while he was on earth. Jesus taught his followers the truth about God – so will the Holy Spirit. Jesus challenged his disciples to recognise the truth about themselves – so will the Holy Spirit. Just like Jesus, this Counsellor will help them to understand God's word, encourage them and support them.

- So the "Counsellor" who comes to live in Christians is the Spirit of Jesus himself. This is what Christians mean when they talk about "the Holy Spirit".

- The Spirit is not some sort of weird impersonal power. Jesus calls the Holy Spirit "him" and "he". The Spirit is a person – in fact He is God – God in your life.

*Note: If your group includes people with little or no Bible knowledge, you may want to give a very quick explanation of the Trinity here. It's enough to explain that the Bible says that **God is one** (there is only one God), but also that **God is three** (God the Father, God the Son, and God the Holy Spirit). Three persons - one God.*

2. The Holy Spirit shows us the truth

- Do you see how Jesus describes the Holy Spirit in v 17? "The Spirit of Truth".

- Our sin blinds us to the truth about God, and to the truth about who Jesus is and what he came to do (his identity and mission).

- Only if the Holy Spirit works in our lives will we start to understand the truth of these things.

- So if you're starting to be convinced that Jesus is who he claims to be – the Son of God – then it's not because you're brilliantly clever, but because God's Spirit is already working in your heart to help you understand it.

- And if you're starting to see that Jesus' mission to die for our sins and rise again is true, then that too is God already working in your heart to show you the truth.

- And if you're still scratching your head and wondering what this is all about, then it's not because you're incredibly stupid. It's because the only way you can understand the truth about God is if the Holy Spirit helps you understand it. You need to ask him to help you understand the truth.

3. The Holy Spirit shows us our sin

- A little later in John, Jesus says this:

▶ *Read aloud* **John 16:8**.

- "When he [the Holy Spirit] comes, he will convict the world of guilt in regard to sin and righteousness and judgment."

- Just as Jesus showed people the sin in their lives, so his Spirit does the same today.

- Do you remember the way Jesus spoke to the rich man – gently pointing out his sin and telling him to build "treasure in heaven" instead? Well that's exactly what the Holy Spirit does in people's hearts today.

- If you're starting to see that you're a sinner who needs rescuing, that shows the Spirit is already working in your life. He's showing you what real goodness – "righteousness" – is, and showing you how far you fall short of it, and how much we need forgiveness.

4. The Holy Spirit gives us the desire to obey God

- None of us naturally has the desire to obey God. You might have realized that from your own experience. That's why we need God's Spirit to change us from the inside out.

- We're going to turn to the Old Testament, to the book of Ezekiel. This is a promise from God himself, to all those who put their trust in him.

▶ *Read aloud **Ezekiel 36:26–27**.*

- So, the Spirit changes people's hearts, taking away stone-like hearts that don't care about God and giving them hearts that desire to obey God. He makes it possible for us to do things that previously would have seemed too hard or that we would simply not want to do ourselves. If you have started to have a longing in your heart to go God's way, then it's a sign that the Holy Spirit is at work in your life. He fights against everything that keeps you from knowing God more fully.

Starting and continuing

- I don't want to give you the impression that this happens all at once. Being a Christian is about growing. Growing in our understanding of the truth about God. Growing in our understanding of the truth about ourselves. And growing in our ability to love God, and live in a way that pleases him.

- Think of it this way. It's a bit like moving into a new house. There's a "moving in day" when you arrive with all your boxes and stuff. Over the next few weeks, you unpack and put all your furniture in the rooms, and your clothes in the drawers. But it's only over a long period of time that you redecorate the house, and make it how you want it. It's like that when you become a Christian – except you are the house and God is the one who moves in! It will take him a long time to change you – and some of the changes you will find incredibly hard. But in the end he is "remaking" you into how he wants you to be.

▶ *You may want to ask one of the leaders (or a Christian group member) to give an example of how the Holy Spirit has affected their life – by teaching them the truth, by showing them their sin, or by giving them a desire to live for God. Give them plenty of advance notice and plan time for them to discuss what they want to say with you or a co-leader beforehand. It is important that they make clear that being a Christian is great, but also tough.*

Conclusion

Now, you might be thinking: "If I become a Christian, I could never change; I could never keep it up; I could never live like I am supposed to." And that's true – you can't. And God knows that too. That's why he sends the Holy Spirit into our lives to help us.

DOWNLOAD

The recap (called DOWNLOAD) below appears in the group member's CY or CY Nano Handbook for their reference.

- The Holy Spirit, who comes to live in Christians, is the Spirit of Jesus himself – the Holy Spirit is God.

- The Holy Spirit helps us in a number of ways including:

  - Guiding followers of Jesus

  - Showing people their sin

  - Changing people so they want to please God (*CY Nano*)

  - Changing people by giving them the desire to please God (*CY*)

- Jesus promises that when we trust in him, he will come and live in us forever by his Spirit (John 14:15-17).

TALKBACK

▶ *Use the questions below to encourage discussion (they are also printed on page 29 in the group member's CY or CY Nano Handbook).*

Before CY (or CY Nano), what did you know about the Holy Spirit?

- Use the opportunity to emphasize the main points of the talk, and to correct any wrong ideas.

What did you find most surprising about who the Holy Spirit is or what the Holy Spirit does?

- Again, this is an opportunity to reinforce or extend some of the teaching from the talk.

How do you feel about the Spirit of Jesus coming to live "with you" and "in you"? (John 14:17)

- Individuals may feel scared about the idea of the Spirit living in them. Reassure them by telling them that he is the "Spirit of Jesus".

- In other words, it is Jesus who comes to live in you with all his goodness, love and forgiveness. He wants what is best for you, and will guide you towards living that way.

- Remind them that the Holy Spirit is the "Counsellor" or comforter or helper. He brings us assurance that we are forgiven, and that we are part of God's family.

SESSION 2: THE CHURCH

GROUP ACTIVITY

▶ *Choose one of the following activities, to suit your group and the time you have available. If your weekend/day away is held somewhere with more space or different facilities than your usual venue, choose an activity you wouldn't usually be able to do.*

CAKE BAKE

Aim: To show the importance of co-operation in the church family.

Equipment: You will need an oven nearby, and the following items gift-wrapped: a cook book with a cupcake recipe; a wooden spoon; kitchen scales; paper cupcake cases; the ingredients needed for the recipe; baking tray; bowl.

- ❯ Tell the group that they are going to bake cupcakes. Give each member one of the gift-wrapped items. Explain that each person is responsible for using their particular item during the making of the cupcakes. They must co-operate with each other since they are not allowed to use another person's item.

- ❯ Ask them to unwrap their item and get baking!

- ❯ Once the cupcakes are in the oven, leave them to bake while you deliver the talk. You can then give the cakes out at the end.

Note: If you want, you can make this activity easier by using a box-kit (available from supermarkets) with ready-mixed ingredients for making cakes or cookies. This would take less time, and almost guarantee something edible at the end of the process!

At the end of the activity, say to participants: "I hope you could see that if you didn't work together, we wouldn't have been able to get the cakes made. In the same way, Christians need to help each other to keep following Jesus."

MULTI-LEGGED RACE

Aim: To show the importance of co-operation in the church family.

Equipment: Fabric strips or scarves to tie legs together.

- ❯ Divide the group into two teams. Both teams need to have the same number of competitors, so include a leader in one team if necessary.

- ❯ Give each team one fewer strips of fabric than there are people in the team.

- ❯ Ask each team to tie their legs together as they would for a three-legged race (eg: groups of five people tied together would make it a six-legged race). This is easiest if they line up side-by-side first, and then tie their legs together.

- ❯ When both teams are ready, have a race to the far end of the room/field and back.

Note: If you have a large group, divide them into three or more equal teams.

At the end of the activity, say to participants: "If you didn't work together, you couldn't have run the race – and you would have found it hard even to stand up! In the same way, Christians need to help each other to keep following Jesus."

MUSICAL MAYHEM

Aim: To show the importance of co-operation in the church family.

Equipment: A set of whistles or handbells tuned to different notes (eg: from "musical Christmas crackers" or toy shops) – alternatively try borrowing chime bars from a local primary school. Simple sheet music.

- Give each group member an instrument, and make sure they know which musical note it plays. If you have more instruments than people, some group members can play two instruments.

- Choose a "conductor" – preferably someone who can read music, although the set of instruments you use may also have an alternative way of showing a tune (eg: if each instrument is marked with a number).

- The conductor points to each person when it is their turn to play. Encourage the group to work together to make the most tuneful sound they can. It might help to try playing a simple scale first, before attempting anything too ambitious!

Note: This activity is best suited to a smaller group so that everyone can take part together.

At the end of the activity, say to participants: "If you didn't work together, and listen to each other, you couldn't have made a very musical sound. In the same way, Christians need to help each other to keep following Jesus."

TALK 2: CHURCH/CY THE CHURCH IS YOUR FAMILY

▣ *This talk must be delivered "live" – there is no material for the Inside Track sessions on the Soul DVD. Deliver Talk 2 using the notes below. The notes for this talk can also be downloaded from www.christianityexplored.org/cy to enable you to adapt them for your group and add your own illustrations.*

▣ *There is a recap (called DOWNLOAD) in the participant's CY or CY Nano Handbook for their reference. Encourage people to write notes on the Download page as they listen to the talk.*

OUTLINE OF TALK 2: CY THE CHURCH IS YOUR FAMILY

▣ *Use the outline below to develop your own talk. This outline can also be downloaded from www.christianityexplored.org/cy*

Aim

- To explain that a church is a family of Christians who meet together.

- To show that we need to help each other if we are to live the Christian life.

- To explain that a good church is where Christians listen carefully to God's word – the Bible – and change how they think and live as a result. They also encourage each other, remember Jesus' death and resurrection, and pray together.

- To show that being part of the church is a great privilege – but sometimes it can also be tough.

Opening

- What springs to mind when you think of church? Maybe you think of a building in the centre of your town, or a Sunday service with lots of old ladies wearing hats, or a place where some people go for a coffee morning now and again. *(You could play the first 1½ minutes of Episode 1 of the Soul DVD here to show some ideas of "church".)*

- But the Bible says church is none of those things. It's a family of people who believe in Jesus.

1. What is a church?

▶ *Read aloud* **Hebrews 10:25**. *(Either stop reading after the words "encourage one another", or continue to the end of the verse and explain that "the Day approaching" means they were looking ahead to when Jesus will come back again on the Day of Judgment.)*

- So the church is about meeting with one another and encouraging each other.

- One of the amazing things about becoming a Christian is that you're immediately part of a family. The Bible often talks about God as our Father and Christians as his adopted children. So, every Christian has a whole bunch of new brothers and sisters who are looking out for them.

▶ *Ask one of the leaders (or a Christian group member) to talk about how the church has been an encouragement to them, and also how going to church has been tough. If you ask a group member, give them plenty of advance notice and plan time for them to discuss what they want to say with you or a co-leader beforehand.*

- Proverbs 13:20 says: "He who walks with the wise grows wise, but a companion of fools suffers harm". This verse is talking about how you can spend time with two different types of people. If you hang out with a fool, the Bible says you'll suffer harm. If you hang out with a wise person, the Bible says you'll grow wise. We need to have Christians around us because they will have a positive influence on us and help us to be wise in living for God.

- So the Christian life is not a solo activity; it's not about going on your own – it's about teamwork.

- It's like the activity we did together a moment ago, where we all had to help each other. Everybody in the church has a role to play, and they need to work with each other so that the whole church benefits and serves God together.

▶ *Give an example from your own life of how being surrounded by like-minded people helps you. For example: training for a race, trying to lose weight, or learning a new skill such as pottery or playing the viola.*

- If you look around the people here, you might think we're a weird bunch! And you might think that at church too. Sometimes it can be tough getting on with other Christians. But that's another thing the Holy Spirit helps us with. He draws Christians together as members of God's family, so we can help and support each other. He helps us to genuinely love each other.

2. What happens at church?

❯ So what's church supposed to be like? In the book of Acts we find out what happened after Jesus died and came back to life. It's like a time capsule because it shows us what the very first churches were like.

▶ *Read aloud* **Acts 2:42**.

❯ The apostles were all men who had spent time with Jesus. This verse tells us that the church "devoted themselves to the apostles' teaching and to the fellowship, to the breaking of bread and to prayer."

❯ What four things happen here? *(Ask the group to suggest answers.)*

> ❯ They listen carefully to God's word (the apostles' teaching) and change how they think and live as a result.

> ❯ They care for one another.

> ❯ They remember Jesus' death by breaking bread (which churches do today when they take communion or The Lord's Supper together).

> ❯ They pray.

❯ It's so important to find a church where all these things happen.

Conclusion

Church should be about people who follow Jesus spending time with one another, encouraging one another and getting to know God better. Being part of a church is a great privilege. Sometimes it can also be tough – but if we ask the Holy Spirit to help us get along together, he will.

DOWNLOAD

The recap (called DOWNLOAD) below appears in the group member's CY or CY Nano Handbook for their reference.

❯ In the Bible, "the church" is not a building – it's a group of Christians who follow Jesus together.

❯ The Holy Spirit unites Christians as members of God's family.

❯ If we're to live the Christian life, we need to help each other.

❯ A good church is where Christians listen carefully to God's word – the Bible – and change how they think and live as a result. They also encourage each other, remember Jesus' death and resurrection, and pray together.

TALKBACK

▶ *Use the questions below to encourage discussion (they are also printed on page 31 in the group member's CY or CY Nano Handbook).*

> **What has church been like for you? Has your experience of church been good or not so good? (CY Nano)**
>
> **What has been your experience of church? Was it positive or negative? (CY)**

- ❯ We need to recognize that many young people will have had an experience of church that is not positive.

- ❯ This is an opportunity to explain why some adult Christians may have been unhelpful or have not worked at communicating the gospel properly as they should. Churches are made up of sinful human beings like you and me, so it is not surprising that it goes wrong sometimes.

- ❯ It may also be necessary to point out that some churches may not be real churches at all. They may have forgotten that Jesus saves them by God's grace, and think that they please God by their services, goodness and religious practices. It is not surprising that these churches may be cold or harsh or irrelevant – because they are not the real thing.

> **What do you think God's family *should* be like?**

- ❯ If the group has caught the vision for what church is for, and could be like, this should provoke a great discussion.

- ❯ If particular grievances about the way your church operates come up, then write them down to discuss later – either as a youth leadership team, or with your church leaders. But make sure that the group doesn't think that they can insist that the rest of the church does things their way. *They* must encourage other Christians, just as much as other Christians encourage them.

- ❯ Young people often respond very positively when given responsibility, so help them see that the church family is a great opportunity to really make a difference in other people's lives, eg: by encouraging younger Christians or serving members of the church family who are elderly or unwell.

> **How do you think a good church will help someone who's trying to follow Jesus? (CY Nano)**
>
> **What difference do you think a good church should make to someone who's trying to follow Jesus? (CY)**

- ❯ It should be the place where we find the love and forgiveness of Jesus, learn more about him and grow to be more like him.

- ❯ Use the opportunity to share your own testimony of how you have been helped by, and enjoyed the opportunity to contribute to, churches you have belonged to in the past. It's important to show how wonderful it is to be part of such a diverse but like-minded family.

SESSION 3: THE BIBLE AND PRAYER

GROUP ACTIVITY

▶ *Choose one of the following activities, to suit your group and the time you have available. If your weekend/day away is held somewhere with more space or different facilities than your usual venue, choose an activity you wouldn't usually be able to do.*

TEAM CHARADES

Aim: To show the importance of being able to speak to others.

Equipment: A list of words that can be acted out; a prize.

- ❯ Split the participants into teams of around 5-6 people each.

- ❯ Announce that you are going to play Team Charades.

- ❯ Explain that one person from each team will come to you to be told a particular word that they are to act out for their team. They must then act out the word without speaking or writing. If someone guesses the word correctly, they run to you and tell you the answer. You then give that person the next word on the list and they go back and act this out to their team.

- ❯ The game continues until one team wins by reaching the end of the list. Award that team a prize.

At the end of the activity, say to participants: "Aren't you glad that you don't have to communicate like that all the time? We're going to think now about how God communicates with us."

SILENT ADVERTS

Aim: To show the importance of being able to speak to others.

Equipment: A data projector, one or more adverts to show.

- ❯ Show the adverts to your group, but with the sound turned off. If possible, stop the advert before the name of the product is displayed. Ask your group if they can guess what is being advertised.

- ❯ Divide the group into small groups of 3-4. Give each group the name of a product that they have to advertise, but without speaking.

- ❯ Give them three minutes to plan their advert. Then each group performs their silent advert for the others, who have to try to guess what it's for.

At the end of the activity, say to participants: "Aren't you glad that you don't have to communicate like that all the time? We're going to think now about how God communicates with us."

CODE BREAKERS

Aim: To introduce the subject of clear communication.

Equipment: Code funsheets or blank paper; pens.

- ❯ A younger group might enjoy working out some secret codes. You could either create your own code sheet beforehand, with a secret message they have to unravel, or give them a message that they have to put in code for another group.

- This can be a quiet activity sat round a table, or made more active by hiding code words around the room.

- Choose relevant Bible verses as the secret messages. These might be verses looked at earlier in the CY or CY Nano course, or perhaps verses that link to the theme of the Bible and prayer (eg: 2 Timothy 3:16-17; Philippians 4:6; 1 Thessalonians 5:16-18). Another option would be to encode Psalm 1, dividing it into sections for the different teams, so that the group is already familiar with these verses before you look at them during the talk.

At the end of the activity, say to participants: "Aren't you glad that you don't have to communicate like that all the time? We're going to think now about how God communicates with us."

TALK 3: TALK/CY IT'S GOOD TO TALK

▶ *This talk must be delivered "live" – there is no material for the Inside Track sessions on the Soul DVD. Deliver Talk 3 using the notes below. The notes for this talk can also be downloaded from www.christianityexplored.org/cy to enable you to adapt them for your group and add your own illustrations.*

▶ *There is a recap (called DOWNLOAD) in the group member's CY or CY Nano Handbook for their reference. Encourage people to write notes on the Download page as they listen to the talk.*

OUTLINE OF TALK 3: CY IT'S GOOD TO TALK

▶ *Use the outline below to develop your own talk. This outline can also be downloaded from www.christianityexplored.org/cy*

Aim

- To show that the Bible and prayer are vital to the Christian life.

- To explain that when we read the Bible, God talks to us.

- To explain that when we pray, we talk to God.

- To show that reading the Bible and praying are great – but we can also find them tough.

Opening

▶ *You may want to use the following illustration (or come up with another illustration that is particularly relevant to your group):*
Good communication is important, isn't it? Some people really aren't very good at it. There was a sign in an office which said: "Would the person who took the step ladder yesterday please bring it back or further steps will be taken". And a sign on a church noticeboard said: "Weightwatchers will meet at 7pm. Please use large double door at the side entrance." *(You can find other examples of mis-communication on signs by searching online for "funny signs around the world".)*

- Good communication is the key to knowing God. We need to speak regularly and honestly with God, and also listen to what he wants to say to us. That's why Christians pray and read the Bible – in the Bible God talks to us and in prayer we talk to God.

1. God talks to us

▶ *You may want to use the following illustration (or come up with another illustration that is particularly relevant to your group):*

Imagine the postman delivers a letter to you. You pick it up and then, if you're anything like me, you look to see who it's from, because when we know who it's written by, it affects the way we read it. If it comes from your friend or is important news, you'd read it really carefully. But if it's a letter from your dentist, or someone you've never heard of trying to sell you chair covers, you'd probably just look it over quickly and then throw it away. But when we pick up the Bible, we should remember that it's a love letter from God and full of important news. So we'll want to read it really carefully.

▶ *Read aloud* **Psalm 1:1–3**.

- Verse 2 tells us that the Christian's "delight is in the law of the LORD, and on his law he meditates day and night". So Christians are to follow, not the people around them, but what God's law – the Bible – says. When we read the Bible, we are reading God's words to us. God talks to us.

- And in case you're worrying that reading the Bible is like trying to understand an astronomy text book written in Russian – that's something else the Holy Spirit helps us with. He helps us to understand the Bible, and to do what God is telling us.

- And as we listen to God's words in the Bible, we become, verse 3 says, "like a tree planted by streams of water, which yields its fruit in season and whose leaf does not wither." It's like one of those great big trees you sometimes see in a forest – it's so big, you can't get your arms around it – it's been there for years. Storms have come and gone but it's still there. And it's still producing fruit – year in, year out. Amazing that it keeps going. But of course, it wouldn't keep going if it had no water. Trees need it to survive.

- And that's what it says here: if we want to be strong and keep going year after year, we need the Bible – just as a tree needs water.

▶ *Read aloud* **Psalm 1:4–6**.

- Did you notice the contrast there? These people, who don't care what God wants to say to them, are like "chaff". That's the useless bits left over at harvest time when the farmer is collecting grain. You know, the husks and bits of straw. And, unlike the tree by the river, they just get blown away by the wind.

- It's amazing to know God "watches over" those who have put their trust in him. But there's a warning that people who ignore the words of the one who made them have no future and will perish.

- So, will we be like chaff – with no stability, or substance, and no future? Or will we be like the tree – firmly rooted and fed and strengthened by what we read in the Bible?

2. We talk to God

❯ It's really hard to communicate with people without using words, isn't it? Some of you were better at it than others when we played the game, but words just make it so much easier, don't they? It's the same if we want to build a relationship with God. We're going to need to talk to him – and that's what prayer is all about.

❯ We're going to look together at one of the prayers in the Bible.

❯ *Read aloud* **Acts 4:23–31**.

❯ Can you think of the worst time in your life, when everything seemed to be going badly wrong? Well, that's exactly where the disciples are at this point. Their two main leaders have just been questioned by the most important religious leaders, who are determined to shut them up. So what's the answer? What's the best thing to do in this situation? Answer: they pray together.

❯ And look at who they pray to in verse 24: the "Sovereign Lord ... [who] made the heaven and the earth and the sea, and everything in them." It's as if they're saying: "Lord, you made the universe, our world and all the people who live in it, and you're in control of everything, even those people who are threatening us."

❯ That's who Christians pray to: a God who is unimaginably powerful, who is the real King of everyone and everything.

❯ However much people try, plotting against this "Sovereign Lord" is a complete waste of time. So even though Herod, Pilate, the Gentiles and the people of Israel all plotted to have Jesus killed, verse 28 tells us: "They did what your power and will had decided beforehand should happen." You have to be incredibly powerful to make your enemies do what you want, even as they're doing what *they* want!

❯ The disciples then ask for God's help. They pray in verse 29: "Now, Lord, consider their threats and enable your servants to speak your word with great boldness." And God responds to their prayer in a very visible way: "After they prayed, the place where they were meeting was shaken. And they were all filled with the Holy Spirit and spoke the word of God boldly."

❯ That's another thing the Holy Spirit helps us to do – he helps us to be bold when we tell people about Jesus. By speaking the word of God boldly, they are doing exactly what the authorities have forbidden them to do. You wouldn't do that unless you believed that God was in control!

❯ Of course, God doesn't always answer prayer in the way Christians want or expect. At moments like that, we must remember that God is still in control; that he has a plan; that he is wiser and more loving than we are; and that the decisions he makes are trustworthy. There will be difficult situations that we won't understand until we're with God in eternity.

❯ So when Christians pray, they're praying to the Sovereign Lord, who is in complete control of everything that will happen. It's an amazing privilege. And it means that Christians can talk to God about anything. He is interested in even the small details of their lives.

❯ When talking to God, you mustn't forget to say the things you'd say to a trusted friend. You'd apologize for the things you've done wrong and ask them to forgive you. You'd thank them, ask them for help (for yourself or for other people), tell them your secrets, and pour out your heart to them.

- The difference is, when you talk to God, you're talking to someone who is in control of everything – and who loves to give you every good thing you need. He even gives us help when we don't know what to say. If you're not sure how to pray, or what to pray about, ask the Holy Spirit to help you. He will!

Conclusion

- What is your attitude to prayer and the Bible? Sometimes people use them as a last resort when everything else fails. There they are on the way to school or college and they've got a really tough exam coming up; they haven't done much studying, so they pray something like this: "Please God, get me through this test and I promise I'll be nice to grandma from now on". And sometimes we treat the Bible in the same way. It's where you go for some emotional support or help in emergencies.

- But praying and reading the Bible shouldn't be like a big red button we press only in an emergency. Actually, it's what Christians do every day because they want to know God better.

▶ *Ask one of the leaders (or a Christian group member) to talk about the importance of speaking to God and God speaking to them through his word. Ask them to include times when they have found prayer and Bible reading tough, as well as ways in which it has been great. If you ask a group member, give them plenty of advance notice and plan time for them to discuss what they want to say with you or a co-leader beforehand.*

DOWNLOAD

The recap (called DOWNLOAD) below appears in the group member's CY or CY Nano Handbook for their reference.

- The Bible and prayer are really important for Christians (*CY Nano*)/vital to the Christian life (*CY*). When we read the Bible, God talks to us. When we pray, we talk to God.

- The Bible helps us to be strong and to keep going in the Christian life.

- Christians can pray to God about anything, knowing that he is in control of everything.

TALKBACK

▶ *Use the questions below to encourage discussion (they are also printed on page 33 in the participant's CY or CY Nano Handbook).*

> **Have you read any parts of the Bible? What did you like about them? What did you find difficult?**

- Encourage the group to mention their favourite story, or Bible passage; tell them yours and why you find it so exciting.

● People may say that they find the Bible difficult to understand. Encourage them to read the Gospels first. Remind them that the Holy Spirit will help them to understand the Bible if they ask him to. Explain too that this is why we have groups like this – to help with some of the more difficult things.

● Some people may raise specific instances of things they find hard to believe. Offer to discuss these with them at some point during the weekend/day.

Do you ever pray? What kind of things do you say to God? When are you most likely to talk to God?

● It's very rare for anyone to say they have never prayed. Listen to the answers carefully. It may then be appropriate to say: "How would you feel if someone treated you like that – if they only rang you up when they were in trouble or they needed something?"; "What would that say about that relationship?"

● You might give the group some examples of how/when you pray, and the kinds of things you pray about (thanks and praise as well as asking for help).

What do you think you might find most difficult about praying and reading the Bible?

● Here are three areas that are worth focusing on:

● *Opportunity:* many young people find it hard to find the space and quiet – especially if they share a bedroom. Make suggestions for when and where they could set aside time to read and pray regularly.

● *Keeping going:* suggest Bible notes, meeting with small groups of friends to pray regularly for each other, etc.

● *Understanding:* suggest an ongoing group Bible study that might be appropriate to them.

It may be useful to have Bible-reading notes available to help anyone in your group who wants to begin reading the Bible for themselves.

It may also help to put a prayer diary together for the group – or to give them a copy of the church prayer diary, if there is one.

CONCLUSION

This talk wraps up the weekend/day away. It is very short and can be given just after the closing session on the Bible and prayer. This talk must be delivered "live" – there is no material for the Inside Track sessions on the Soul DVD.

▶ *Deliver the Conclusion using the notes below. The notes for this talk can also be downloaded from www.christianityexplored.org/cy to enable you to adapt them for your group and add your own illustrations.*

OUTLINE OF CONCLUSION

▶ *Use the outline below to develop your own talk. This outline can also be downloaded from www.christianityexplored.org/cy*

Aim

❯ To recap the main points covered during the weekend/day away.

❯ To prepare the group members for session 7, the final session of the CY & CY Nano course.

❯ To challenge group members to think about the personal implications for them if they follow Jesus.

Talk

❯ Being a Christian is both great and tough. We've seen examples of this from the lives of the very first Christians, and we've also heard examples from leaders *(and group members)* who are living as Christians right now.

❯ We've thought about the things God gives us to help us live for him:

   ❯ *The Holy Spirit* – who shows us our sinfulness and helps us to change on the inside and want to live for God.

   ❯ *The church* – meeting together with other Christians who help us keep going as followers of Jesus.

   ❯ *The Bible and prayer* – God talks to us through his book, the Bible, and he helps us talk to him, too, as we pray.

❯ In the closing session of the *CY / CY Nano* course we will be looking at exactly what it means to be a Christian. To help us be ready for that session, I'm going to give you two questions to think about. I'm not going to ask you the answers today, but it will help if you think about them before our last meeting together.

❯ The questions are:

   1. What sort of things would you need to start doing if you followed Jesus?

   2. What things would you need to stop doing if you followed Jesus?

❯ We've seen that God will help you as you start doing some things and stop doing others – he'll help you by his Spirit, through other Christians in the church, and as you read the Bible and pray. God will help you – but it's still important to think carefully about the difference being a Christian will make to you personally. So that's why we're asking you to think about these two questions before we meet again.

❯ We'll pick up some of your answers in the last session as we think about exactly what it means to be a Christian.

PRAYER

It may be appropriate to end your weekend/day away with the following prayer. Up to now in the CY / CY Nano course we haven't included any prayers. This is because it's important not to embarrass people by putting them in uncomfortable positions, or to assume that they are happy to take part in a prayer to God, when they may not be convinced that he exists. However, prayer is an important part of the Christian life. It is also an opportunity for Christians to model the relationship that we can have with our heavenly Father because of Jesus.

If it would be appropriate for your group, do use the following prayer (or a similar one of your own) to end this final session of your time away. Explain to the group beforehand that you are going to thank God for the weekend/day away you have enjoyed together. Explain that, if they would like to join in with this prayer, they can do so by saying "Amen" at the end, which means: "We agree".

> **Heavenly Father, thank you for the time we have spent together this weekend *(today)*, for the fun we've had, and the time to get to know each other better. Thank you that we now know more about what it's like being a Christian – and the things you give us to help us. Please help us to think carefully about the difference it would make to each of us if we followed Jesus. And help us to understand that it's not only tough but also wonderful to be a Christian. Amen.**

AFTERWARDS

- Did any of the group members say they would like to find out more, attend another course or join a church group? If so, plan how you will follow that up, as well as praying for that person.

- Did any of the group seem confused or worried about the role of the Holy Spirit? Think about how you might help them further.

- Thank God for all those who came on the weekend/day away, and for giving you the privilege of spending more time with them.

- Pray for those who have said they would like to start using Bible-reading notes. Plan to get some notes to them soon if you haven't already given them some notes to start with.

- Pray for the final session coming up and plan how you will use the prayer at the end.

- Plan your follow-up for the whole group.

Questions
(and answers)

Answering tough questions

OPEN TO QUESTION

One of the most important aspects of running a course like CY is that it encourages participants to ask questions in an environment where they will be taken seriously, and not be ridiculed or belittled. You should encourage your group with words like: *"No question is too simple, or too difficult – CY is about you finding answers to the important questions of life."*

It is this atmosphere of open enquiry that encourages young people to "open up" about spiritual things, and to approach the Bible, not as a dead textbook, but as the source for answers. It is your job to help create this environment by your openness, honesty and willingness to talk in a relaxed way about things that group members may find particularly difficult to articulate.

WHY PEOPLE DON'T ASK QUESTIONS

There are a number of reasons why people won't ask questions:

- **Because they don't have any!** Particularly for younger teens, it may be that they have not yet developed to the stage where they have questions about spiritual things. It may be they are from a Christian home, and have not yet started to question the things they have always been taught, or that they are simply not interested. The good news is that at some stage they will probably start to think more deeply, and the word of God often provokes reactions and questions. So in the course of reading Mark, they are likely to come up with some. And if they are part of a larger group that is dealing with questions, then they will be encouraged to join in. *Don't force the issue – let them develop in their own time.*

- **Because they are bored or don't care!** It's possible that some young people in your group may be there because they "have to be"; for example, if they are a regular member of your group and are in church because of family expectations, or have come for the friendship and activities, rather than the Bible. Again, don't despair. Pray for them, think of ways that you can make it more engaging for them, but don't let their apathy suppress the interest and enthusiasm that other group members may be showing.

- **Because they are frightened of appearing stupid.** This is a BIG issue for many people, especially young people. If they think the question is simple, or that they will be belittled by others for asking it, then they will not speak up. The key here is to

make sure you keep repeating the words: *"No question is too simple, or too difficult –*
CY is about you finding answers to the important questions of life."

- ⦿ **Because they are shy.** Some people just aren't good at speaking up in groups. And that is fine. Just make sure that you are able to talk with them personally about their questions. Watch out for the tell-tale signs of a wrinkled forehead as they read or listen.

- ⦿ **Because they need time.** Some people just need more time to get to the question. They may think of something later that evening or during the next week. So you should always give an opportunity to deal with questions from the previous session that have occurred to people, and don't make them feel that everyone is taking a step backwards because "all that was dealt with last time."

WHY DO PEOPLE ASK QUESTIONS?

It might seem obvious: "Because they want to know the answer" – but it often runs much deeper than that:

- ⦿ **Because I want to test you.** The precise question they ask may not be of particular concern to them. It could just be that they have heard it expressed by others, or know that it is a tricky question for Christians to answer. What they are more interested in is how you handle it (see below). By not being rattled, and by taking the question seriously and demonstrating that you have given it some thought, you are answering "the question behind the question", which is "Are these people trustworthy?" *Always take questions seriously.*

- ⦿ **Because I genuinely don't understand.** There may be a huge variation in Bible knowledge in your group, and some will want to ask what you might consider to be really basic questions: "Who was Jesus?", "When did all this happen?", "What is prayer?" etc. Again, treat them seriously, and make sure the rest of the group do not look down on those with less knowledge than they have.

- ⦿ **Because I have had a distressing personal experience.** There is a world of difference between someone asking: "Why does God allow suffering" as an academic question, and someone who asks the same question having watched a close relative die of cancer recently. The way you answer the two may be completely different. And of course, you will not know if others listening in to your answer are carrying a burden of disappointment or personal pain. *Always answer compassionately.*

- ⦿ **Because I have been let down.** The way a question is phrased may be the key to getting an insight here. So instead of "What is prayer?", asking "Why does God answer some prayers and not others?" may indicate that the questioner has some specific disappointment in mind. Similarly, a question about Christians being hypocrites may relate to some bitter personal experience of a Christian or a church in the past. *Always answer honestly.*

- ⦿ **Because I want to know you respect me.** Many teenagers and young people have a love/hate relationship with older generations. They want to rebel, but they also want to be accepted and respected. The way you treat their questions, their ideas and their opinions is often as important as the substance of your answer. *Answer respectfully.*

- ⦿ **Because I want to be sure it all makes sense.** The interest in a particular question may not be because it is a problem, but rather that they are seeking a sense that the Christian faith as a whole sticks together coherently. So answering in a way that connects the question with the big picture of the Bible's message is important. *Answer from the Bible, not just from sensible reasons or philosophy.*

HOW DO I ANSWER?

The following two appendices give you some suggested approaches to answering the substance of the difficult questions that people ask. But, as we have suggested above, it is equally important that we answer in the right way. 1 Peter 3:15-16 says:

> But in your hearts set apart Christ as Lord[1]. Always be prepared[2] to give an answer to everyone who asks you to give the reason[3] for the hope that you have. But do this with gentleness and respect[4]...

Notice 4 things about giving answers:

1. **The person who answers the questions needs to be someone who is personally committed to the lordship of Christ.** This is important, because the answer to their unspoken questions is not your arguments or knowledge – it is your life. Many of their most important questions will remain unarticulated, like: *"Is this relevant to me?"*, *"What does this look like in a real person?"* and *"Could I be a Christian?"* All these questions are answered by the way you live and model being a disciple and follower of Jesus. Are you fun to be with, are you displaying the joy, peace, love and contentment in life that comes from knowing Christ as Lord? If you come to CY feeling resentful, angry and doubtful in your own standing with God, then you cannot hope to influence your group members for the gospel. They may hear convincing arguments from your mouth, but your life will speak much more loudly.

2. **You must be ready to answer.** Take time to think through the answers on the following pages, and come to your own conclusion about them. You should be as sure in your answer as the Bible is – no less, no more! For example, on the questions of the origin of evil, or the reason for suffering, we do not have final and complete answers from the Bible, and therefore, we must be careful in what we say and acknowledge our difficulty with these issues, rather than insisting that we have it all sewn up.

3. **You must have a reasonable answer.** In other words, saying "Just have faith in the Bible" is not enough – even if we cannot prove it with complete certainty, we have to show the *reasonableness* of our faith.

4. **You must answer gently and respectfully.** Even (perhaps especially) when people are hostile, we must model kindness, love and fairness in our attitudes, thinking and speaking. Only in this way will we win people for the gospel.

MORE TIPS ON ANSWERING QUESTIONS

- **Involve the group.** Resist the temptation to answer the question on your own. It is good practice to first ask: *"Does anyone else find this a difficult question?"* You can then address your answers to the whole group. It may also be that you have Christians in your group who will be able to help answer. So you might ask: *"Has anyone in the group got an answer to that?"* In this way you are also training and encouraging the Christians to get involved in the discussion. It has been the experience on many Christianity Explored courses that involving the group in answering questions often helps other "not-yet-Christians" start to see the wrong thinking in some of their doubts as they start to argue back with a questioner!

- **Go to the Bible.** The Bible is the sword of the Spirit, so we must have confidence that if we direct people to its answers, God will do his work through it. If you can, go to a Bible passage to read and then explain, especially if it is in Mark's Gospel.

- **Empathise.** Don't give the impression that you have everything sewn up. If you have wrestled with this question in the past – tell them. If you still have areas that you wrestle with, say so, but also tell them why it is no longer a problem in the larger scheme of your faith. For example: *"I find suffering (eg: a natural disaster such as a major earthquake) very difficult to understand, but I know that God weeps over it too and cares, because he sent Jesus into the world, and he has experienced the pain and suffering of our broken world."*

- **Give them time.** Don't assume that they will sort out everything right at that moment. Many of the ideas and arguments and thoughts from the Bible will take time to sink in and be processed. Leave the question open for another day, and encourage them to think about it seriously over the next week, eg: *"There are some big things to think about there, and you might not feel this discussion has answered all your questions immediately, but can I ask you to think about it, and maybe we can return to it next week if you want to go into it in more depth."*

AND FINALLY...

Don't be afraid to admit that you don't know the answer to a question. But do promise to find out before the next session.

Questions from Mark's Gospel

MARK 1:2-3
What are these strange quotes at the start?
Mark quotes from the Jewish Bible (what we call the Old Testament) – Malachi 3:1 and Isaiah 40:3 (written 600 years before Jesus was born). They are quotes from passages that promise a messenger who will announce the arrival of a rescuer King – the Christ or Messiah who will save God's people from judgment. The promise of a messenger is clearly fulfilled by John the Baptist in Mark 1:4–8. Even his clothing (Mark 1:6) was like that of an Old Testament prophet, in particular Elijah (2 Kings 1:8).

MARK 1:13
What are angels?
The word literally means "messenger". They are spiritual beings in the service of God, who particularly are sent to deliver messages. An angel delivers the wonderful message of the resurrection in Mark 16:5-6. He is described as looking like a young man dressed in a white robe. No mention of wings!

MARK 1:23-27
What are evil spirits and demons?
The Bible says that there is an unseen spiritual world, which includes angels and evil spirits. According to the Bible, Satan, or the devil, is a fallen angel who is in rebellion against God and hostile to God's people. Demons are part of that fallen spiritual world, and serve Satan. Although Satan and his demons are powerful, the New Testament shows that Jesus has overcome Satan by the power of his death on the cross (see Colossians 2:15).

Note: If this topic comes up, deal with it briefly but don't allow it to dominate the session – teenagers will be fascinated by "the dark side" and want to talk about it for hours. And make sure you explain to them that Christians have nothing to fear from the devil – Jesus has defeated him.

MARK 1:34; 7:36
Why did Jesus tell the people he healed not to tell anyone?
No one has ever healed people as Jesus did. It was instantaneous, spectacular and complete. People didn't just "start to feel a bit better". They were completely better straightaway. Not surprisingly he drew huge crowds who wanted to see these amazing miracles, but who seemed less interested in his teaching. Jesus did not want people coming just to see signs and wonders. He rejected such people (Mark 8:11-13). In Mark 1:45 it becomes clear that he has to leave the crowds in order to teach. He probably told people not to tell anyone so that the crowds would not become a problem.

MARK 2:10
Why did Jesus call himself the Son of Man?
"Son of Man" is a Jewish term meaning simply "a man". But "Son of Man" is also a well-known title used in the Old Testament for the Messiah – God's promised King. See Daniel 7:13-14. The religious leaders would have understood that Jesus' use of the title "Son of Man" was a claim to be the Messiah.

MARK 2:16
What is a Pharisee?
This group of strict Jews did not just obey the Old Testament but held to many strict traditions. They were seen as some of the most holy men in Israel. But Jesus called them "hypocrites", which literally means "play-actors," because of the way they showed off their religion and self-righteousness. He strongly condemns them in passages such as Mark 7:6-9.

MARK 2:19
Who is the "bridegroom"?
Jesus is making the point that, for the disciples, fasting (going without food) is totally inappropriate when he's with them, just as it would be for wedding guests to be miserable at a wedding. Jesus is saying he is the bridegroom of God's people. This is another claim to be the Messiah promised by the Old Testament (Isaiah 54:5; 62:4–5; Hosea 2:16-20).

MARK 2:21-2
What is the new cloth/old coat, new wine/old skins story about?
People complained that Jesus was not following the religious rules of his day (Mark 2:18). Jesus says that the faith he has come to bring is not about rules at all. Jesus cannot be "fitted into" their "religion of rules". He came to bring a living friendship with God, not rules. Jesus brings grace, love and peace, not religious rules.

MARK 2:23
What is the Sabbath?
The Sabbath is the special day of rest taken when no work was done. The Sabbath was an opportunity for God's people to remember God's creation and how he rescued them from Egypt.

MARK 3:6
Who are the Herodians?
These were supporters of Herod Antipas, the King of Judea, who depended on the controlling Roman Empire for his power. They would have seen Jesus as a threat to Herod's rule.

MARK 3:13-19
Why did Jesus choose twelve apostles?
Jesus calls the twelve apostles on a mountainside. In the Old Testament God shows himself to his people on mountains (eg: Genesis 8; Exodus 19; and 1 Kings 18). There were twelve tribes of Israel – God's people in the Old Testament. Jesus is making the point that God is calling a new group of people to himself.

MARK 3:22
What does it mean to be possessed by Beelzebub?
Beelzebub is another name for the devil. Note that the religious authorities don't question whether Jesus is powerful or whether the miracles happen. They simply ask where his power comes from. They say that Jesus is possessed by the devil and is driving out demons. Jesus replies that their claim is stupid – after all, if the "prince of demons" really was driving out other demons, then he would be fighting against himself.

MARK 3:29
What is the blasphemy against the Holy Spirit that will never be forgiven?
The religious leaders have seen Jesus perform wonderful miracles, and have heard his astonishing teaching. Now they claim that the work of the Holy Spirit is actually the work of the devil. Jesus' warning has nothing to do with swearing at the Holy Spirit – in simple terms, it means rejecting the only way of forgiveness that God has provided. Of course, this sin is only unforgivable for as long as a person goes on committing it. Many of the same religious leaders changed their minds about Jesus later, and so were forgiven (Acts 6:7). This is vital to understand. There can be no forgiveness if we reject Jesus.

MARK 4:2
Why did Jesus teach in parables?
Jesus told these memorable stories to teach spiritual truths. Parables have a clear surface meaning, but also a deeper meaning (often just one main point), which Jesus explains to those

who will listen (Mark 4:1-34). There is a spiritual principle here: "To everyone who has, more will be given" (Luke 19:26). The disciples are intrigued by the parables and draw nearer to Jesus to hear the explanation. But, to the crowd, the parables are just curious stories. They hear, but do not understand (Mark 4:12). All people are like moths or bats. They are either attracted to Jesus' teaching, or repelled by it.

MARK 4:40
Why does Jesus say: "Do you still have no faith?"
Despite all the evidence they've seen, the disciples still don't have faith in Jesus (note: to "have faith" in someone means to trust him or her). The disciples express terror rather than trust both before and after Jesus acts. Interestingly, just before this miracle, Jesus has told three parables making the point that God's word is powerful. He then calms the storm with a word. The disciples should have drawn the obvious conclusion.

MARK 6:3
Did Jesus have brothers and sisters?
These were the natural children of Joseph and Mary, conceived after the birth of Jesus. See also Mark 3:32. This answers the question as to whether Mary remained a virgin after the birth of Jesus. In addition, Matthew 1:25 certainly implies that Joseph and Mary had a normal sexual relationship after Jesus' birth.

MARK 6:7-11
Why did Jesus send out the twelve disciples?
Jesus sends out the twelve, telling them to expect some to accept and some to reject their message. They are to reject those who, by refusing to listen, reject them. The reference to shaking off dust refers to what Jews did on returning to Israel from Gentile countries, which they viewed as "unclean." For the disciples to do it in a Jewish village was like calling the village Gentile! It is a mark of judgment (see also Acts 13:51).

MARK 6:14-29
Why is there all this stuff about John the Baptist?
Mark tells us about the death of John the Baptist to make an important point. It answers the implied question of Mark 6:1–13: *Why don't people see who Jesus is?* The answer is that people reject Jesus because, like Herod, they will not repent. In other words, they will not turn from their rebellion against God.

MARK 7:24-30
Why does Jesus call this woman a dog?
Mark tells us this incident to show that Jesus has come to rescue and save Gentiles as well as Jews. The woman is a Gentile (=non Jew) from near the city of Tyre. "Children" here refers to the Jews, and "dogs" was a common, unflattering expression that Jews used for any Gentile person. So Jesus is saying: "It isn't right to take what belongs to the Jews and give it to you Gentiles." In her reply (v 28) the woman is saying; "Yes Lord – I acknowledge that as a Gentile woman I have no right to ask help from you, the Jewish Messiah. But you have such great power and mercy that you must have enough to help me as well!" Jesus is impressed by her faith and her persistence, and grants her request

MARK 8:15
What is the yeast of the Pharisees and Herod?
Yeast – the stuff you put in bread to make it rise – is used as a picture in the New Testament to refer to the bad influence of someone or something. Just as a tiny amount of yeast has a great effect on the whole batch of dough, so Jesus warns against being affected by the sinful attitudes of the Pharisees and Herod: specifically, these would be hypocrisy and worldliness.

MARK 8:17-21
Why do the disciples not understand?
Jesus has fed thousands in the desert (twice), healed people, forgiven sin, cast out demons and stilled storms with a word. What's wrong with the disciples? As the next two stories show – they need spiritual help to understand what is staring them in the face. Spiritual truth can only be revealed by God's Spirit.

MARK 8:22-25
Why is there a two-part healing?
Jesus hasn't lost his touch, or found it difficult to heal this man. He is doing the healing as a kind of "acted parable" to show what happens next. When Peter announces that Jesus "is the Christ" in Mark 8:29, he is like the man in Mark 8:24 (he has partial sight). It is clear from the verses that follow – where Peter rebukes Jesus – that although he has understood who Jesus is, he has not yet realized why Jesus has come (Mark 8:30-33).

MARK 8:32-33
Why does Jesus say "Get behind me Satan!"?
Peter had recognized that Jesus was the Christ, but he could not understand why Jesus had to suffer and die. Jesus recognizes in Peter's words a temptation to reject God's plan that the Christ should endure the cross. It is not that Peter is Satan, or that Satan has "taken control". It is just that Peter is saying what the devil wants, which is to knock Jesus off course in his mission to rescue us by dying on the cross and rising to life again.

MARK 9:1
What does Jesus mean when he says that some "will not taste death before they see the kingdom of God come with power"?
This probably refers to the transfiguration of Jesus, recorded immediately after (Mark 9:2-7), although it could also be a reference to the coming of the Holy Spirit on the day of Pentecost (Acts 1:8).

MARK 9:4
Who are Elijah and Moses?
Both of these people represent the Old Testament: Moses was the law-giver and Elijah the greatest of the Old Testament prophets. The fact that they talk with Jesus demonstrates that he is the one the Old Testament is pointing to.

MARK 9:11-13
What does Jesus mean when he says "Elijah does come first"?
The disciples have failed to recognize that John the Baptist was the Elijah-like messenger promised in Malachi 4:5-6 who would be the forerunner of "the Lord." Elijah was a prophet in the eighth century BC, who lived out in the wilderness, wearing animal skins and a leather belt (2 Kings 1:8). This is how John the Baptist is described in Mark 1:6. Jesus makes it clear that John was the fulfilment of the prophecy concerning Elijah.

MARK 9:43-48
Why does Jesus tell us to cut our hands off?
Jesus obviously did not intend that a Christian should physically cut off a hand or foot, or pluck out an eye. Jesus is exaggerating to make a point: "If anything is stopping you from entering the kingdom of God, it is better to take drastic action to rid yourself of it, whatever it is, than to end up in hell forever." The most important thing is getting right with God. The logic is obvious: temporary pain is better than eternal punishment.

MARK 10:1-12
What does Jesus think about divorce?
Jesus makes it clear that divorce is always against the perfect purpose of God. God's plan in creation is that married people should live together for their whole lives (see Genesis 2:24). Jesus says that if people seek a divorce because they have found an alternative partner, such action is adultery (Mark 10:11-12). It is only because people's hearts are so hard (Mark 10:5) that divorce could ever be permitted. The danger is either that we use the concession of verse 5 as an excuse for deliberate sin, or that we think that divorce cuts us off from God forever. Christ came to die for all sin, including the failures of divorce.

Note: Be aware that you are likely to have teenagers and young people in your group who have experienced the reality of broken marriages. For some this may be a significant personal issue.

MARK 10:15
What does it mean to "receive the kingdom of God like a little child"?
The disciples need to understand that they have nothing to offer God, and must therefore depend fully on God, just as a little child depends fully on its parents. Jesus' phrase here does not imply innocence or purity – neither of which are traits of most children!

MARK 10:38
What did Jesus mean when he said: "Can you drink the cup I drink..."?
In the Old Testament, "the cup" was generally a reference to suffering. It also refers to the cup of God's anger (see Jeremiah 25:15-16). In verse 38, Jesus is showing that the disciples don't know what they are talking about. They, unlike Jesus, have their own sin to deal with and therefore cannot suffer God's wrath on other people's behalf; a sinless substitute is required. However, Jesus adds – in verse 39 – that they will suffer.

MARK 11:12-14, 20-21
Why did Jesus curse the fig-tree?
This can seem strange as it is Jesus' only destructive miracle. Mark interweaves the cursing of the fig-tree with the events in the temple (Mark 11:15-19, 27-33). In the same way that Jesus curses the fig-tree for having no fruit on it, he condemns the "fruitlessness" of Israel's religion (ie: lack of genuine worship, failing to recognise Jesus as the Messiah etc).

MARK 12:1
What does the story about the vineyard mean?
The vineyard was a common Old Testament symbol of Israel. In particular, this passage is very similar to Isaiah 5, where the people of Israel are rebuked for the terrible way they have rejected God, and are told that God's righteous judgment will come. Jesus' hearers would have understood that the "man" in the parable was God, that the "vineyard" was the people of God, and that the missing fruit was allegiance to the Son.

MARK 12:10
What is a capstone?
This is the most important stone; the foundation stone. Here it means that although Israel's leaders have rejected Jesus, he is still the Messiah, and will become the Saviour through dying on the cross.

MARK 12:18-27
What's the point of the strange "one bride for seven brothers" story?
In Jesus' day there were two major religious groups: the Pharisees, who believed in life after death, and the Sadducees, who said that death was the end. So the Sadducees came up with this question to trick Jesus. In his answer to them, Jesus says two things. First, there *is* life beyond the grave, but no married relationships in heaven. Secondly, he makes it clear that because God is the God of the living, and is referred to as "the God of Abraham, Isaac and Jacob" it must mean that Abraham, Isaac and Jacob are still alive!

MARK 13:14
What is "the abomination that causes desolation"?
This is an example where a parallel passage helps! Luke 21:20 substitutes the words "Jerusalem surrounded by her armies," for this phrase. It refers to the occasion in AD 65 when Roman armies surrounded Jerusalem after a political uprising. After a horrific five-year war, the Roman armies entered the city, desecrated the temple, and then proceeded to pull it down and destroy the city. Jesus' words in Mark 13 came true.

MARK 13:32
Why did Jesus not know the date of his own return?
Some suggest that Jesus could not be perfect, or God, if he does not know this important fact. When Jesus was born as a man he "emptied himself" (Philippians 2:7). As a child, Jesus had to grow in wisdom, just as all human children do. He was not born with complete knowledge built-in. This is one of those things which verifies the

truth of the Bible. If someone was making up the story of Jesus Christ, he would never have left in Mark 13:33!

MARK 14:12
What are "the Feast of Unleavened Bread" and "the Passover lamb"?

God commanded Israel to keep the annual feasts of Passover and Unleavened Bread to remind them of how he had rescued them from slavery in Egypt (Exodus 12:14-20). Israel could only be saved from the tenth plague, the plague on the firstborn, by killing a lamb, eating its roasted flesh with bitter herbs and unleavened bread, and smearing the blood on the door frames. When the angel of death saw blood on a door, he "passed over" the house and spared the firstborn (Exodus 12:1-13). The meal eaten in Mark 14:12-26 takes place at Passover. Jesus' death would be the true means of rescue from God's judgment; it would be the true Passover. This is why Jesus is sometimes referred to as the Lamb of God.

MARK 14:24
What is the "blood of the covenant"?

Not only did Passover commemorate rescue from slavery in Egypt and from the wrath of God by the pouring out of blood (Exodus 12:23), but that rescue was followed by a covenant (an agreement made by God on behalf of his people) that was sealed by a blood sacrifice (Exodus 24:6). Jesus' sacrificial death mirrors this. He bled and died to turn God's wrath away from us and to start a new covenant.

MARK 15:33
Was the darkness an eclipse of the sun?

Not possible. Jesus was crucified at the time of the Jewish Passover, which is always at full moon. At full moon, it is impossible to have a solar eclipse. Physically there is no adequate explanation of the darkness, other than that it is a supernatural sign at the time of mankind's darkest deed – killing the Son of God.

MARK 16:9-20
Why do we stop reading at Mark 16:8? – Most scholars agree that Mark's Gospel ends at chapter 16:8. The women run away terrified, not knowing what to think after being told that Jesus is risen. The ending provokes the question: Are you able to see who Jesus is, why he came, and what it means to follow him?

Verses 9-20 of Mark chapter 16 appear to be attempts by later writers to add a fuller resurrection ending to Mark. However, the oldest manuscripts do not include this section and its style and vocabulary are different from the rest of Mark. This does not mean that what is contained in this ending is made up. Most of the details also appear in the other Gospels. It just means that they were probably not in Mark's original.

Questions about Christian belief

HOW DO YOU KNOW THAT GOD EXISTS?

- There are many philosophical and scientific arguments that you can get involved in, that might show that belief in God is rational, even sensible. But these arguments lead to belief in some kind of creator, not specifically to the God of the Bible. It is usually much better to talk about Jesus and his claim to be God.

- We know God exists because He came to earth in Jesus. This is the substance of Jesus' answer to Philip's question in John 14:8-9 (it's worth looking this up and reading it if the question arises).

- "Have you ever seen God?" "No, but I might have if I'd been born at the right time. If I had been alive 2000 years ago, and living in Palestine, I could have seen God."

- Jesus claimed to be God (eg: John 5:18; 20:28-29) and his actions bore out that claim. If you'd been there, you would have seen and heard him. Check out his claims as you read through Mark and come to CY.

- Believing in God is not "the easy option". If he is God, then you must serve him as God.

WHY SHOULD WE BELIEVE WHAT THE BIBLE SAYS?

- Try not to get involved in defending passages that can be interpreted in a number of different ways. The best place to start is with the reliability of what the Gospels teach about Jesus, and then go on to his teaching and claims on our lives.

- Historical evidence in the New Testament is confirmed at a number of points by non-Christian writers, eg: Tacitus and Josephus.

- The New Testament documents were written soon after the events they describe.

- This New Testament documentation is extensive, coming from as many as ten authors, eight of whom wrote independently of each other.

- The documents are historical in character as well as theological. They contain many verifiable details of the time and culture in which they were written.

- The text of these documents has come down to us intact from the era in which it was written.

- The writers were people who suffered and died for what they believed, and were also of very high moral standing. They believed in telling the truth. It is highly unlikely they would make up these stories, or even "imagine" them.

- The Gospels are less than complimentary to the disciples who wrote them – another sign that they were not made up.

- We have good historical reasons for trusting that what we read in the Gospels is an accurate account of what Jesus did, said and claimed for himself.

- The next step is to work out what you think of Jesus – everything else flows from that.

DON'T ALL GOOD PEOPLE GO TO HEAVEN?

- What is "good"? How "good" is good enough?

- Some of us are better than others but no one meets God's standards (see Romans 3:23).

- We are not good, because our hearts are "sin factories", Mark 7:21-22.

- People who rely on their goodness are deluded (Mark 10:17-22). There is always more we must do. We need rescuing.

- God is after friends, not "good" rebels. It's a matter of whose side you are on.

- The opposite is, in fact, true. Good people go to hell; bad people go to heaven. Those who think they are good and rely on that will be lost. Only those who know they are lost are able to receive forgiveness and eternal life from Christ.

WHY WOULD A GOOD GOD SEND PEOPLE TO HELL?

- God is utterly holy and good. His character is what decides right and wrong in the universe.

- God must judge everyone. He will judge fairly and well.

- Jesus is the most loving person who ever lived, but it is he who teaches most about the reality of hell. He does so because he knows it is real, and doesn't want us to suffer the inevitable consequences of our rebellion against God.

- Heaven and hell are defined by *relationship.* Heaven is enjoying all the good gifts of a Father, and being with him. Hell is the absence of him and his gifts – friendship, love, beauty etc.

- God has judged his Son Jesus on the cross. He went through hell, so we don't have to!

- If we understood how holy God is, we would be asking the opposite question: How can God allow anyone into heaven?

IF GOD FORGIVES EVERYTHING, DOES THAT MEAN I CAN DO WHAT I LIKE?

- God's grace is utterly free. Shockingly, he will save even the worst kind of criminals you can think of.

- Jesus saved a condemned thief who died on the cross next to him!

- If we properly understand how sinful we are, and how our sins have, literally, wounded God; and if we understand how amazing it is that Jesus died for us when we don't deserve it – then we want to live in a way that pleases him.

HOW CAN WE BE SURE THAT THERE IS LIFE AFTER DEATH?

- People may come up with strange stories about "out-of-body experiences" but these prove nothing, and can lead to confusion.

- The Bible says that Jesus' resurrection is the pattern for our own resurrection (eg: 1 Corinthians 15:20).

- Who do you trust for accurate information about life beyond the grave? The person who has been there and come back.

- If Jesus has been raised from the dead, then we will certainly be raised from the dead, and we must look to Jesus' teaching for answers to the questions about what life beyond death will be like.

WHAT ABOUT OTHER RELIGIONS?

- Sincerity is not truth. People can be sincerely wrong.

- If the different religions contradict each other (which they do at several major points), they cannot all be right.

- The question really is: Has God revealed himself, and if so, how? Jesus claimed to be the unique revelation of God. He claimed to be God in the flesh. Are his claims valid? If Jesus is God, the other religions are wrong.

- Jesus claims he is the only way: John 14:6.

- Religions can do many good things – provide comfort, help, social bonding etc. But they are man-made ideas about God, and generally teach that we must DO something to get right with God.

- Jesus claims that his teaching is revealed from God (John 8:28), and that his followers must abandon what they think they can DO, and rely on what he has DONE on the cross to bring forgiveness and new life to them.

WHAT ABOUT THOSE WHO HAVE NEVER HEARD ABOUT JESUS?

- We can trust God to be just; he will judge people according to their response to what they know.

- Everyone has received some revelation, even if only from the created world (see Romans 1:18-19).

- Those who have had more revealed to them will be held responsible (Matthew 11:20-24).

- You have heard – so you must do something about it – and leave the others to God, who will treat them fairly.

ISN'T FAITH JUST A PSYCHOLOGICAL CRUTCH?

- There are different questions here, like: Do I just believe because my parents believe? Or: Do I believe because I have the need for some comfort from above? Or: Do I believe because I have had this or that experience?

- If our faith is based purely on experience ("Christianity works for me"), then there is no way of arguing against this objection. It might work because it's true or because of my particular upbringing or conditioning.

- However, Christianity is based on objective historical events (the death and resurrection of Jesus), and invites people to investigate and test them. The truth of Christianity has nothing to do with our state of mind.

- The same could be applied to any belief – including atheism! (ie: I'm an atheist because my parents were; I have a deep need to be independent; I have had no experience…). None of this helps to establish whether belief in Christianity is based on truth or error.

WHY DOES GOD ALLOW SUFFERING?

- We can't know for sure why God allowed evil into the world.

- Much suffering is a direct result of our own sinfulness (eg: that caused by drunkenness, greed, lust, etc.).

- But some is not (see John 9:1-2).

- All suffering results from the fallen nature of our world (see Romans 8:18-25).

- God uses suffering to discipline and strengthen his children (see Hebrews 12:7-11; Romans 5:3-5).

- God also uses suffering to awaken people to understand that there is a judgment coming to our pain-filled world (Luke 13:1-5).

- God knows our pain. He has done something about our suffering. Jesus suffered and died so that we could be forgiven and become part of the "new creation" where there will be no suffering. Jesus' death for us is the undeniable proof that God loves us.

HASN'T SCIENCE DISPROVED CHRISTIANITY?

- Most people mean: "Hasn't the theory of evolution replaced creation and so disproved Christianity?" People usually are not talking about archaeology which, incidentally, backs up the Bible at almost every point.

- Start by asking what they mean by the question. They may have some specific point that needs addressing and that will requires some research.

- Avoid having a technical discussion about evolution, carbon dating etc.

- Ask what conclusion they are drawing from evolution. It *may be* a description of how life has appeared on earth (although you may want to dispute that!). But it does not answer the bigger questions: *who* and *why*.

- Did the world come into being by chance? How God made the universe is not as important a point as that he made it.

- Steer the conversation towards talking about God's existence (see above) and towards Jesus. If Jesus is God, it puts the creation/evolution debate in a completely different perspective.

IF JESUS IS GOD'S SON, HOW CAN HE BE GOD TOO?

- Jesus describes himself as the "Son of God" – a term which can mean that he is the King of God's people, but can also be a claim to being much more.

- Jesus acts as God does in the Old Testament. He speaks as God speaks, and does things that only God can do (raises the dead, forgives sins, controls nature, etc.). His words and actions show that he is making a claim to be God.

- Christians do not believe that there are many Gods, and that Jesus is just one of them. Christians believe that there is one God – who is a trinity. One God, three persons – the Father, the Son and the Holy Spirits in a relationship of love and service with each other.

- This is complex and hard to completely understand – but why would we expect to fully understand God anyway?

WHY DOES GOD HATE SEX?

- He doesn't. He invented it and thinks it is beautiful, wonderful and powerful.

- God knows best how we work, and his pattern for sex – between a man and a woman in a committed lifelong marriage – is the way he designed it to work best.

- Sex joins people together in a way that is more than physical. If we use sex in other ways, we will inevitably damage our ability to enjoy sex in the way it was intended.

- It may not appear damaging to enjoy this gift in other ways, but we must trust our Maker that it is.

CHRISTIANS ARE HYPOCRITES – SO HOW CAN CHRISTIANITY BE TRUE?

- The failure of many Christians to live according to their stated beliefs does not invalidate Jesus' claims to be God.

- The Bible says that Jesus alone is perfect, and it is honest about the failures and weakness of his followers. The disciples in Mark are constantly making mistakes.

- Jesus taught that there will always be false teachers and fakes (Mark 13:21-22) who pretend they are Christians but who are not. This is true today.

- Everyone is a hypocrite in some sense. But Jesus calls those who follow him to change and grow more like him. Don't be discouraged if you have met some Christians who are not yet perfect. They never will be this side of eternity.

ACKNOWLEDGEMENTS...

This second edition of the *CY* material was edited by Tim Thornborough and Alison Mitchell, building on the original CY material from the first edition, and the *Soul* DVD scripts written by Nate Morgan Locke.

The first edition was developed by Barry Cooper, Matthew Seymour, Sam Shammas and Rico Tice in association with Young Life (UK), ably helped by Ruth Chan, Joanna Cook, and Bob Willetts.

Literally hundreds of people have helped shape *CY* and *CY Nano*, not least through the great feedback we have had from the thousands of leaders and young people who have used *CY* already, and have been kind enough to give us their comments.

Special thanks to our panel of youth leaders and the bright cookies at Christianity Explored who have commented on the revisions as we have gone along: Johnny Beare, Mark Birri, Nicole Carter, Paul Chelson, Martin Cole, Catherine Currell, Ali Harper, Simon Heather, Rachael Holyome, Helen Morrow, Ian Roberts, Matt Simper, Darin Stevens, Luke Thompson, Dave Thornton, and Anne Woodcock.

Dashing designs by André Parker and Steve Devane.

Supporting downloads available from www.christianityexplored.org/cy

⊙ **Talk outlines** – Copies of the talks for the 7 main sessions and for the Inside Track weekend/day away are available as both pdfs and in Word format, so that you can personalise each talk with your own illustrations etc.

⊙ **Visual aids** – A number of visual aids can be downloaded to show during the talks.

⊙ **Resources for activities** – CY and CY Nano include a wide range of optional group activities to use during the sessions. Handouts, quiz questions, diagrams etc can be downloaded to help your preparation. Powerpoint presentations are also available for some activities.

⊙ **Extra ideas** – If none of the suggested activities in the Leader's Guide suit your particular group or situation, you will find a selection of alternative activities available to download. There are also suggestions for extra illustrations you may want to use to help your group understand key teaching points.

⊙ **The Mark challenge** – This outline for reading the Gospel of Mark in three weeks is printed at the back of the CY and CY Nano Handbooks. If you want to challenge your group members to read through Mark's Gospel in this way, but don't want them taking their books home between sessions, you can download the challenge sheet from the website and print as many copies as you need.

⊙ **Feedback form** – You may find it helpful to use a feedback form at the end of the course, both to find out how helpful the course was and also to discover what your group members would like to do next. A sample form is available on the website in a variety of designs and sizes.

⊙ **Soul DVD trailers** – If you are going to show the Soul DVD during each session, then you may like to use a trailer as a way of inviting people to join. There are three trailers available on the DVD. These can also be downloaded from the website.

⊙ **Logos for your own invitations** – If you are going to create your own printed invitations to the course, you can download copies of the CY, CY Nano and Soul logos, which are available in a number of formats.

⊙ **Other recommended resources** – Looking for something to help you or a course participant with a particular issue? You'll find a huge range of recommendations, information and ideas on the website.